THE ROYAL
WEDDING ALBUM

THE ROYAL WEDDING ALBUM

CELEBRATING THE MARRIAGE OF
HRH PRINCE WILLIAM OF WALES
& CATHERINE MIDDLETON

Daily Mail

CONSTABLE

The publishers would like to thank Anna Walton, Lisa Hagenmaier and Paulo Silva
for their help in accessing photographs from the *Daily Mail* archives

Constable & Robinson Ltd
3 The Lanchesters
162 Fulham Palace Road
London W6 9ER

First published in the UK in 2011 by Constable,
an imprint of Constable & Robinson Ltd,
in association with the *Daily Mail*

A copy of the British Library Cataloguing in Publication Data is available from the British Library

ISBN 9781780331744

Designed by Smith & Gilmour, London
Printed in the UK by Scotprint.

All photographs supplied from the Daily Mail Photo Archive except for the following: p8, p75,
p57 top left Tim Rooke/Rex Features; p55, p124 Nils Jorgensen/Rex Features; p73 top left SAC
Faye Storer/Rex Features; p66 top Michael Dunlea/Rex Features; p44, p157 bottom left Ikon
Pictures Ltd/Rex Features; p159 top left & right Richard Young/Rex Features; p21 Alan Davidson/
Rex Features; p96 Reginald Davis/Rex Features; p159 bottom right Rupert Hartley/David Hartley/
Rex Features; p20, p22, p49 top right, p54, p57 top right & bottom right, p152, p154 top, p159
bottom left Rex Features, p171 © PA Images

CONTENTS

INTRODUCTION

While this book is, essentially, a celebration of a romantic event, a royal wedding, that has lifted the spirits of a nation beset by depressing stories of economic gloom and natural disasters it is also a record of a historic event. Prince William will one day become king and Catherine Middleton will be his queen.

There are very few newspapers that can claim to have been at the forefront of world affairs in three different centuries, not only reporting the news but also participating in historic events and setting records in the process, but the *Daily Mail* is one of them. Founded in May 1896, the fledgling *Daily Mail* was intended to have a print run of just 100,000 but was so successful that the initial printings were almost four times that amount, rising steadily over the next few years until, when it reported the end of the Boer War in 1902, over a million copies were being printed every day – the highest newspaper circulation in the world at that time. Today the *Daily Mail* sells over 2 million copies a day, the third largest English-language daily newspaper circulation in the world.

Photographs had been used in the most advanced newspapers for around ten years before the *Daily Mail* came into existence, and the new newspaper was quick to grasp the importance of photo opportunities, relying heavily on the skill of its photographers to be able to capture a moment when they found themselves, either by chance or by design, in the right place at the right time. One of the most iconic photographs of the Second World War was taken by *Daily Mail* Chief Photographer Herbert Mason on the night of 29 December 1940. During the height of the Blitz, when German bombs were raining down on London, Herbert was on fire watch on the roof of the *Daily Mail* offices in Carmelite Street, running between Fleet Street and the Thames. By the light of a thousand fires he could see thick smoke drifting above sheets of flame not far to the east of his rooftop station. Then, as a curtain of smoke briefly parted, he saw the dome of St Paul's standing proudly and defiantly amid the inferno. He raised his camera and captured a moment that was to inspire the nation.

St Paul's had been hit by incendiary bombs, but the flames were successfully extinguished by brave and resourceful fire fighters. Had it been reduced to rubble, as many of the buildings around it were, it would have been a serious blow to the country's morale. It would also have meant that at least one of the weddings featured in this book would have reverted to the more traditional venue of Westminster Abbey. In a break with convention, Prince Charles and Lady Diana Spencer were married at St Paul's. Their wedding, as with every other royal occasion since the *Daily Mail's* inception, was comprehensively covered by the newspaper's photographers, but even in the relatively modern times of 1981, press photographers were still using cameras loaded with film. Digital cameras were under development, but were a long way from producing the kind of clear, crisp images in the user-friendly manner that we have all come to expect nowadays.

In contrast, the wedding of Prince William and Catherine Middleton was beamed live around the world to an estimated TV audience of 2 billion and digital photographs were flashed in an instant via laptops and internet links straight from the photographers' cameras to the newspaper editors' computer screens. The *Daily Mail* had photographers positioned at strategic points to cover the entire pageant and the photographs they took will join the 25 million images held in the newspaper's photo archive; another slice of history to add to the newspaper's catalogue of life in the 19th, 20th and 21st centuries.

CHAPTER I
THE BRIDE
MISS CATHERINE ELIZABETH MIDDLETON

Her wedding is the bride's day, or so they say, and she should be the centre of everyone's attention, the one everyone most wants to see, the one who receives all the gasps of admiration. That, of course, is how it normally works out. The bride arrives for the ceremony looking radiant and beautiful in a gown that ensures all eyes are on her. She dazzles the assembled guests, and captures the focus of the photographer's lens. This is not usually too difficult a task: even when dressed in their Sunday best, the guests never outshine the bride; however, a royal wedding is different. With a wealth of ceremonial splendour on display, colourful uniforms decked with medals and, practised pageantry providing a magnificent spectacle, it takes a very special bride to claim the day as her own. Catherine Middleton has shown over the past few months that she has the fortitude to do just that.

Born five months before her future husband, on 9 January 1982 at the Royal Berkshire Hospital in Reading, Catherine Middleton is the eldest of Michael and Carole Middleton's three children. The day before Prince William was born, Catherine, who would become known as 'Kate', was christened at St Andrew's Church in Bradfield, her home village in Berkshire.

When she was just two years old, Kate and her sister, Pippa, who was then only eight months old, moved with their parents from the green and leafy county of Berkshire to the dry and dusty climate of Amman in Jordan, where their father would work for the next two-and-a-half years.

Kate went to nursery school in Amman from the time she was three but once the family were back home in England she went with Pippa and their mum to the 'mothers and toddlers' playgroup in St Peter's Church Hall in Bradfield. She then graduated to the pre-school nursery, eventually attending Bradfield Church of England Primary School, starting in 1986. Just as Prince Harry would follow Prince William through school, Pippa followed Kate and the two girls developed a wide range of friends in the local area, becoming very much a part of the village

Top: Kate next to the birthday girl at her friend Angharad Allford's first birthday

Bottom: Kate, in the centre of the front row, as St Andrew's School's highest scoring rounders player

kids' network, especially when they had a baby brother, James, born in April 1987.

Kate and Pippa both joined the Brownies at St Peter's and thoroughly enjoyed Brownie life that involved going to camp where they mucked in with the other girls by peeling potatoes and washing dishes as well as joining in with all of the activities, from swinging on ropes in the adventure play area to bottle-feeding lambs on farm visits.

In 1989 Kate was enrolled at private prep school, St Andrew's School in Pangbourne, just a short car journey from home. She worked hard in the classroom, always showing good progress with her schoolwork, but Kate really shone when it came to sports, playing netball and hockey, tennis, rounders, basketball and just about any other sport she was given the opportunity to try. She also enjoyed drama, and took part in a number of school pantomimes and plays, including the starring role as Eliza Doolittle in a production of *My Fair Lady* when Kate was just ten.

When Kate was thirteen her parents moved to Chapel Row, near Bucklebury in Berkshire but Kate had only a short time at the family's new home before she was off to boarding school at Downe House, not far from Bucklebury. Kate spent only a couple of terms there, however, before she was on the move again, this time to Marlborough College in Wiltshire. Originally established in 1834 as a boys' school, Marlborough became co-educational in 1989 and today around a third of its 870 pupils are girls.

Although she was a good student and multi-talented when it came to sports, Kate lacked confidence. She was tall, slim and athletic, yet Kate's contemporaries at Marlborough remember her as being awkward and shy at first. She was certainly homesick, missed her family and chose to spend a great deal of time closeted in the Elmhurst boarding house (one of the all-girls houses) where she would study alone.

Teenagers, of course, go through all sorts of phases as their hormones put their emotions through the equivalent of a washing machine's fast spin cycle, and the Kate who had starred in plays

Opposite clockwise from the top: Kate, far left, in St Andrew's School uniform summer dress; celebrating victory with the St Andrew's School hockey team; back row, centre, playing Goal Defence for the St Andrew's School netball team; competitive swimming at St Andrew's with Kate back row, third from left; close up of Kate in her school uniform

and taken part in public-speaking contests at St Andrew's had not shrunk from view forever. Many of Marlborough's students were the well-heeled children of well-connected, high society families and Kate may have felt a little in awe of her upper crust associates at first, but she slowly began to fit in with school life, becoming captain of the hockey team and playing in the first pair at tennis. Neither was her academic work shown to be lacking: Kate studied hard to achieve 11 GCSE passes, following them up with three A-levels in chemistry, biology and art. On top of all that, Kate also completed her Duke of Edinburgh's Gold Award while at Malborough. The Duke of Edinburgh's Award is a tough test of character that requires dedication and stamina to undertake a series of activities that include voluntary work, sport or other physically challenging activities, a skills-based challenge and a period of work undertaken as part of a team staying away from home. Earning the credits required to win the Gold Award means putting in the effort every week to keep your personal programme moving forward over a period of at least a year. It's no mean feat to be able to claim the award while still a teenager. The Gold Award is for those in the sixteen to twenty-four age bracket and many choose to complete it long after they have left school, with the stress of A levels far behind. Completing the award while still at Marlborough shows that Kate displayed real determination.

During her final few terms at Marlborough, Kate had blossomed into a vivacious, outgoing, beautiful young woman and the boys at school had certainly started to take notice. Kate's name has been mentioned alongside those of two or three young men but she had never had a serious boyfriend and at this point she had more on her mind working out how to fill her gap year before immersing herself in university life.

In September 2000, while her little sister returned to Marlborough for her penultimate year there, Catherine travelled to Florence where she was enrolled on a three-month course to study Italian at the British Institute. Florence is home to some of the world's most important art collections, including the Uffizi,

Top and bottom: Messing around with friends at Marlborough College

which holds works by Caravaggio, Michaelangelo, Giotto, Titian and Leonardo da Vinci and the Galleria dell'Academia which houses Michaelangelo's David. The route to the city and the trails around its galleries are well-worn by British art students and it is a popular destination for those intending to take art at university.

As well as studying Italian and viewing the art collections in Florence, Kate was able to indulge another artistic passion: photography. At various times there had been discussions about her possibly turning to photography as a career and she was later to put her skill with the camera to good use by working on catalogues for her parents' business.

While in Florence, Kate shared a flat with a group of girls and enjoyed lively evenings in local bars and restaurants although, just as they had done at Marlborough, her friends later maintained that Kate never became outrageously drunk – as so many of them did – but remained in control, making one or two glasses of wine last her the whole evening. At Marlborough, when some of the students sneaked booze into school to celebrate their exam results, Kate was said to have joined in for a time but then volunteered to keep lookout for teachers prowling the corridors.

Home in time for Christmas, Kate planned out the next few months in preparation for her first term at St Andrews University in September 2001. She would take a summer break with her parents, as had become traditional for the Middleton family, in Barbados, but she also managed to fit in a spell in Southampton sailing as a crew member aboard Round the World Challenge yachts in the Solent. By strange coincidence, although it is far from unusual for Duke of Edinburgh's Award winners to do so, she also spent several weeks on a Raleigh International operation in Chile, missing her future husband on his own visit there by just a few weeks.

At St Andrews, Kate quickly became fully involved in university life, having fun at the traditional 'Raisin Weekend' fancy dress foam fight and representing the university on the hockey team. She lived in the St Salvator's halls of residence,

Top and Bottom: More fun at Marlborough

on the floor above Prince William (the halls of residence are split into single-sex stories) and the two soon became part of the same circle of friends. They had a great deal in common: they had both been to exclusive public schools; they had both suffered the anguish of homesickness as boarders; they both enjoyed skiing, sports and outdoors pursuits; they were both studying art and, most peculiarly, they had both spent time over the previous months on voluntary work in Chile.

Kate knew that William was dating another girl for a few weeks during their first term at St Andrews, but that did nothing to stop the pair from becoming firm friends. Over the coming months, Kate and William would see the nature of their relationship develop into something entirely different. Catherine Middleton would soon become the most talked-about young woman in the country.

Kate joins in the traditional 'Raisin Day' foam fight at St Andrews University

Following pages: Kate at the Cheltenham Festival in 2007; at a fundraising event for the Starlight Children's Foundation in 2009; at the Spirit of Christmas Festival at Olympia in 2005

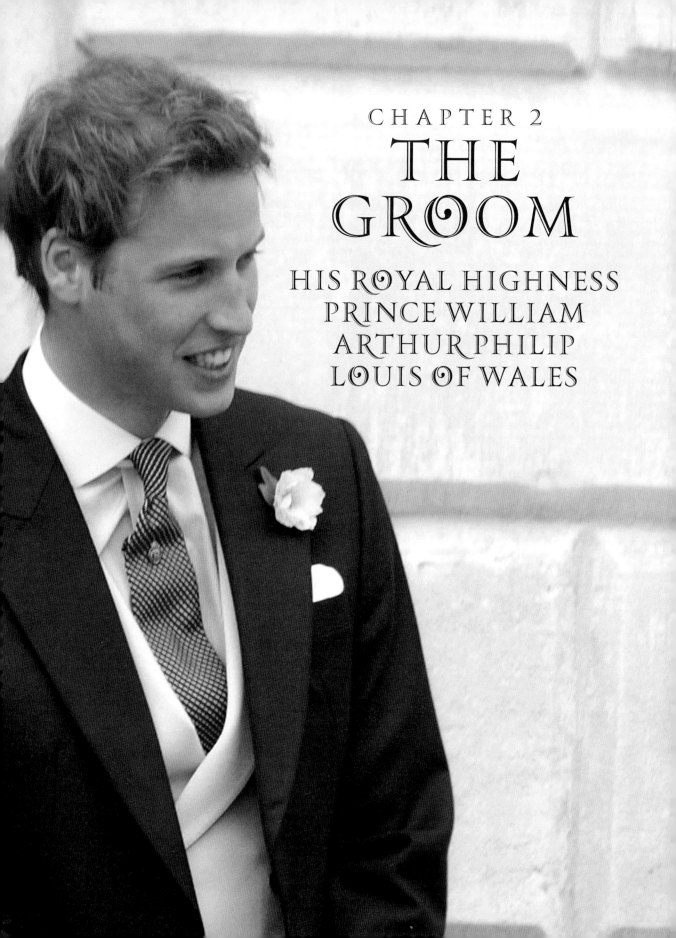

CHAPTER 2
THE GROOM

HIS ROYAL HIGHNESS PRINCE WILLIAM ARTHUR PHILIP LOUIS OF WALES

The second eldest grandson of The Queen (his cousin Peter Philips was born in 1977), and second in line to the throne after his father, Prince William was born at St Mary's Hospital in London on 21 June 1982. He was christened by the Archbishop of Canterbury in the music room at Buckingham Palace on 4 August 1982. William was dressed in the Honiton lace gown that has traditionally been used for the christening of royal babies ever since Queen Victoria had the gown made for her first child, Princess Victoria, in 1841.

Prince Charles had a reduced diary of royal duties during 1982 so that he could be there while William was growing up for those first few months; both Charles and Princess Diana were, however, scheduled to visit Australia and New Zealand for a busy, six-week tour at a time when William was still only nine months old. Although it went against the best advice of the Foreign Office, Diana insisted that William should accompany them on the twenty-seven-hour flight and during their subsequent engagements wherever possible. She made it clear that she was not prepared to be separated from her infant son for such a long time. William went with his parents and embarked on what would become a globetrotting lifestyle before he could even walk.

William was two years old when his brother, Harry, was born in September 1984. Although he is said to have had a little trouble sharing either his possessions or his parents' affection with the new arrival, just like any other older sibling, William grew to become quite protective of his younger brother. Harry was certainly a welcome playmate and the two spent hours together in the nursery at Kensington Palace. Their mother often joked, however, that they were no angels. While visiting the Light Dragoons in Germany – Diana was their Colonel-in-Chief – in 1993, the princess took only Harry with her and explained to one of the army wives she met that, 'If I had brought them both, they would have fought over the tanks.'

Just as there had been a break with tradition in William accompanying his parents to Australia, there was also something

Previous spread: Princes Harry and William at the wedding of Prince Charles and Camilla Parker-Bowles

Opposite clockwise from top left: Charles and Diana bring the baby prince home from St Mary's Hospital, Paddington; William in his mother's arms; on tour in Australia with his parents in 1983; going walkabout in his snowsuit at Kensington Palace, December 1983; arriving at Aberdeen on an aircraft of The Queen's Flight en route to Balmoral in August 1983

of a sea change when it came to William's education. Young royal children were usually educated privately, at home. Diana was determined that William and Harry should mix with children of their own age, so he was sent to Jane Mynor's Nursery School in Notting Hill Gate, the young prince arriving for his first day in a blaze of publicity. There was no way to hide from the press and the public the fact that William was attending the nursery school, but discreet security measures were put in place to ensure the protection of the future heir to the throne: bulletproof glass had been installed in the building; William's police-protection officer was in attendance when he went to school; and other armed police officers were also never far away.

William progressed from Jane Mynor's to Wetherby School, close to his old nursery, in 1987. He was a more disciplined boy than he had been only a few months previously at his Uncle Andrew's marriage to Sarah Ferguson, where he had repeatedly poked his tongue out at anyone he found watching him, including millions of TV viewers. He was also reported to have been displaying tantrums and, while any child of four or five can be expected to act up from time to time, William's bad behaviour was increasingly blamed on the breakdown of his parents' relationship. Prince Charles was then spending the majority of his time at Highgrove, while Princess Diana was at Kensington Palace with William and Harry. The family would generally be reunited at weekends in the country at Highgrove, although the atmosphere was far from relaxed when his parents were both around.

Charles and Diana were with eight-year-old William when he was taken to Ludgrove School in Berkshire for the first time. Ludgrove was a boarding school and William would return home only once a month, as well as during school holidays. Even phone calls home were strictly limited to 'emergencies only'. William was very unhappy for the first few weeks at Ludgrove and Diana travelled regularly to the school to comfort and reassure him. It wasn't long, however, before William started to take a full and active part in school life. He became captain of the rugby

Opposite clockwise from top left: Horseplay at Balmoral with little brother, Harry; playing with a dog is more fun than watching polo, June 1986; first day at Jane Mynor's Nursery School in September 1985

Following pages: Prince William on his way home to Kensington Palace after his first day at nursery; playing on the old estate fire engine at Sandringham, January 1988

and hockey teams, played football and basketball, was a star swimmer and represented the school as a cross-country runner. William made many friends and it was while larking around playing golf in 1991 that he was rushed to the Royal Berkshire Hospital, having accidentally been whacked in the head with a seven iron. He had a depressed fracture of the skull and had to be operated on at Great Ormond Street Hospital in London. He has a scar on the side of his forehead to remind him of his golfing injury.

After the summer holidays in 1992, William's brother joined him at Ludgrove and the two boys were glad of each other's company. Although the press had been persuaded not to pester William and Harry at school, stories about the state of their parents' marriage were splashed across the tabloids on a daily basis. Most boys like to keep their school and home lives strictly separate, so they can be who they want to be at school and revert to being who they are expected to be at home; however, despite the many privileges William and Harry had enjoyed throughout their young lives, keeping their home life at arms' length from their school life was a luxury that was to be denied them. It is tough for any child when their parents split up and when their friends hear that their family life has been turned upside down. It must be unimaginably tough for a child when the Prime Minister announces their parents' separation in the House of Commons before the whole world, as happened to William and Harry on 9 December 1992.

William had been doing well at Ludgrove, both academically and on the sports fields, but his work slipped back for a while after his parents parted company. He worked his way back to good form again, however, and despite further revelations about his parents' private lives over the next couple of years, he kept a cool head and passed the entrance exam for Eton College, moving to the prestigious school in 1995.

Eton was another break with tradition for this generation of royal students. His father and grandfather had both attended

Opposite clockwise from top left: William as the innkeeper in his first school nativity play, 1986; playing football at Wetherby School, 1989; arriving for his first day at Ludgrove School, September 1990; with his mother and brother at church on Christmas Day, Sandringham, 1991; Princess Diana greets her sons aboard the Royal Yacht Britannia, Toronto 1991; fun at Thorpe Park, 1991; first day at Wetherby School, January 1987; on holiday on Richard Branson's Necker Island in 1990

Gordonstoun, a school in the northeast of Scotland renowned for its tough discipline, hardy regime and lack of creature comforts. Prince Charles had not enjoyed his time there and wanted something different for his sons. Princess Diana and he were, on that matter at least, in complete agreement. Both Diana's father and brother were Old Etonians.

Eton had been a school for boys since the fifteenth century, when it was founded by King Henry VI. Nestling by the River Thames near Windsor, the school has produced a host of influential figures, including nineteen British prime ministers, David Cameron being one of them. Eton is supported by a wealth of history and tradition, but is well known as a thoroughly modern and forward-thinking establishment. William was very pleased to be going to Eton College.

The close proximity of the college to Windsor Castle also meant that William could spend time with his grandparents when The Queen was in residence there. They regularly had tea together on a Sunday afternoon, when The Queen gently advised him about what lay ahead for him as the future king. She also used the time to catch up on everything that was going on in her grandson's life.

As they had done at Ludgrove, in return for a handful of updates and occasional interviews, the press left William alone. He captained his house team at football and put his skill as a swimmer to good use playing water polo, but also kept up with his studies. He was to leave the school with A levels in geography, biology and history of art. Before then, however, fate was to deal him the harshest blow of all.

On 31 August 1997, while William and Harry were asleep at Balmoral where they were holidaying with their father, Prince Charles was given the news that Princess Diana had been seriously injured in a car accident in Paris. It was 1 a.m. and the Prince decided to let his sons sleep as he would have more information to give them in the morning. He waited by the phone in his study. Two hours later he was informed that Diana had died.

Previous spread: Prince William on his first day at Eton

Opposite clockwise from top left: William and Harry on their way to a party with Princess Diana; former World Champion Racing Driver Jackie Stewart shows William round a Formula 1 car before the British Grand Prix at Silverstone in 1992; at Wimbledon for the Ladies Final in 1991; skiing at Lech in Austria with his brother and mother in 1991

Princess Diana's funeral took place on 6 September. The day before William and Harry, accompanied by their father, viewed the floral tributes which were piled several feet deep around the gates to Kensington Palace. With a polite nod or a quiet 'thank you' William acknowledged the heartfelt commiserations of the hundreds of mourners who had gathered to pay their respects.

The following day, William stood tall beside his uncle, the Earl Spencer, waiting on The Mall to walk behind his mother's coffin on its slow journey from St James's Palace, through streets lined with mourners and on to Westminster Abbey for the funeral service. Only fifteen years old, William was already significantly taller than his father and grandfather, and Harry had yet to catch him up, so it was William and Diana's brother who stood out as the chief mourners, maintaining a dignified demeanour throughout the procession.

While most students wait nervously at home to hear the results of their A-level exams, William left the country to begin a gap-year tour by jetting out to Belize where he joined the Welsh Guards on a jungle training exercise for a few days. He ate army field rations and slept in a hammock slung between two trees – it was here that he heard the news about his A-level passes, but he didn't rush home to celebrate.

Instead, he was off to Tortel in southern Chile to join the Raleigh International volunteers, working with the educational development charity as a teacher. He lived with a group of other young teachers in basic accommodation, sharing the chores in the evenings and teaching children during the school day. During the ten weeks that William was in Chile, he also undertook manual labour, hefting logs to help construct walkways and enjoying an active outdoor lifestyle.

William also spent time during his gap year working on a dairy farm in England, up before dawn for the milking and never shirking on the mucky jobs, all for a wage of just £3.20 per hour.

Opposite clockwise from top left: William arriving with his family for his first day at Eton in 1995; at his mother's funeral in 1997; following Princess Diana's coffin into Westminster Abbey; happier times, skiing with Prince Charles in Klosters, 2000; with his uncle, brother and father as Princess Diana's funeral cortege passes by

William had already decided that he would take up the offer of a place at Scotland's oldest university, St Andrews, when his gap year was over. When it was announced that he would be going to St Andrews, the number of applications from prospective female students soared so anxious were they for the chance to meet one of the world's most eligible bachelors. William was to begin his university career studying for an art history degree and, just as they had done while he had been at school, the press agreed to leave him to his work. During his first term at the university, William stayed in the St Salvator's halls of residence on the campus, but took great pains to ensure that his arrival would not spoil the university experience for other students. Nevertheless, a crowd of around 4,000 gathered to watch as Prince Charles drove his son to the campus on 23 September 2001.

William was not there for Freshers Week and did not take part in the Raisin Weekend festivities in November which traditionally end with a shaving-foam fight in the St Salvator's quad; he seemed determined to keep a low profile. In fact, by spring 2002, William was having serious doubts about university life and had long conversations with his father about whether he should continue with his course. He was, no doubt, feeling a great deal of pressure to remain at the university. It would be very bad publicity for the Royal Family if the future king dropped out of university in his first year. In the end, the dilemma was resolved by William switching courses to study geography instead of art history. Instrumental in helping him make that decision was someone who he had recently met, a student who lived on the floor above him at St Salvator's and had become part of his close circle of friends – Catherine Middleton.

Previous spread: William and Harry playing polo in 2009; William riding an off-road motorbike in South Africa in 2008

Opposite clockwise from top left: Photocall at Highgrove, 1999; sampling food and drink with Prince Charles on a visit to Wales, 2003; enjoying the South versus North rugby match at Twickenham, 2005

CHAPTER 3

A ROYAL ROMANCE

PRINCE WILLIAM AND CATHERINE TOGETHER

During their first couple of terms at the University of St Andrews, there was no hint of romance between William and Catherine. They knew each other and, especially during the second term when William began to participate a little more in university life, they spent a good deal of time in each other's company. There was speculation in the press about the prince's love life whenever any young woman was seen within arm's reach of him but those within their circle of friends knew there was nothing of that nature between William and Catherine.

William had been anxious to protect the image of the Royal Family by being careful not to make an exhibition of himself in public and had, consequently, led a rather quiet life during his first term at university; however, he slowly began to make a few changes. He started playing rugby again, and football, and joined the university's water polo club. He began to go out more and was seen with his friends enjoying a few drinks in bars and clubs such as Ma Bells. He was even reported to be dating a young lady, Carly Massy-Birch, although they were said to have been 'an item' for only a short time.

Kate, meanwhile, was thoroughly enjoying university life, helping to establish the Lumsden Club, which aimed to stage parties and events throughout the year to raise money for women's and children's charities. She had also met a law student in his final year at St Andrews, Rupert Finch, and the two were said to be dating, although any budding romance appears to have been short-lived.

When Catherine and William returned to St Andrews after the Christmas break, William had settled any doubts he'd had about continuing at university and was seen out and about far more. One of those occasions was at a charity fashion show where Kate was one of the models. William paid £200 for a front-row seat and was delighted to see Kate modelling a dress (actually originally intended to be a long skirt) designed by Charlotte Todd and made from delicately-woven see-through silk. The outfit,

Opposite top: Princes William and Harry arrive with their uncle, Prince Andrew, for the Queen's Golden Jubilee thanksgiving service at St Paul's Cathedral in 2002

Opposite bottom: On the processional route to St Paul's for the thanksgiving service

and the model, stole the show. When the dress came up for auction in March 2011, the scrap of silk that had cost around £30 to make was sold for £78,000.

In their second year at St Andrews, William and Catherine decided, as many students do, to move out of the halls of residence and find a flat to rent in town: along with another couple of friends, Fergus Boyd and Olivia Bleasdale.

William had known Fergus, a solicitor's son from Wiltshire, since they had played rugby together at Eton; they were now both part of St Andrews' water polo team. Fergus had also been one of Kate's fellow models at the previous term's fashion show, although he had not caused quite the sensation that Kate had.

Olivia Bleasdale, was, like Kate, also studying art history, and together the four friends moved into a flat in a Georgian terraced house in the old part of St Andrews town. Their new lodgings were as anonymous as any other student-occupied flat, except that there were rather more police patrols cruising down their street and parked surreptitiously nearby, and security officers who kept a discreet watch on the young man who was second-in-line to the throne.

The group shared the chores around the flat and tried to set up a cooking-and-cleaning rota, although William later admitted that it all went hopelessly wrong quite early on. Despite the cooking lessons he'd had at Eton, his culinary skills were not of the highest standard and all four were generally busy with classes, sports and other activities. They tended to eat out a lot or send out for takeaways. These aren't always viable options for the run-of-the-mill impecunious university student, but the four friends came from families who were rather better-heeled than most.

Neither is it usually a student's privilege to be invited to join a select shooting party of sixteen friends for a weekend in Norfolk, but that's where Kate found herself late in 2002. Prince William was hosting the weekend at Wood Farm near Sandringham. By then, Kate's relationship with Rupert Finch was a thing of the past and she and William had begun to spend ever more time in each other's company.

Opposite clockwise from top left: Kate in the famous dress at the charity fashion show at St Andrews University; William relaxing for a photocall on the beach at St Andrews; William and Harry with their grandparents for the Trooping of the Colour ceremony in 2003; William accompanies his father on a trip to North Wales in 2003

In May 2003 they attended a ball together at Kinkell Farm in Fife, organised by St Andrews' Kate Kennedy Club, of which William was a member. The club, which Kate Middleton's all-girl Lumsden Club had been set up to shadow, was traditionally a male-only institution, it's aim being for the members to enjoy themselves thoroughly while raising money for good causes. Those who were present at the ball thought that Kate and William were acting far more like a couple than just flatmates.

Shortly thereafter, Kate watched Willliam play rugby in a late-season seven-a-side tournament, again sparking speculation that these two friends had now become a couple.

Kate's twenty-first birthday celebrations were postponed from the start of the year until she was back home at her parents' house in Berkshire for the summer. A marquee was set up in the garden and friends from Marlborough and St Andrews were invited to join the celebrations. The guest of honour was Prince William. Although he did not stay long, his presence undoubtedly set tongues wagging. When William celebrated his own twenty-first birthday a couple of weeks later the guest list included royalty, celebrities and friends, including a contingent from St Andrews. Kate's presence at the African-themed party, which hit the headlines when an eccentric would-be comedian gatecrasher dressed as Osama Bin Laden breached security to hijack the proceedings, went almost unnoticed. William, quizzed by the press who noted the attendance of several supposed 'old flames', denied having a girlfriend and claimed to be enjoying being single. He also expressed concerns about how any girl he might become involved with would cope with being hounded by the press.

When they returned to university in the autumn, the four flatmates had new accommodation, moving to Balgove House, a farmhouse in the countryside within easy striking distance of St Andrews. Here they could enjoy the peace and quiet of a rural setting, while still being only minutes away from the bustle of the university town. It was also easier for the Prince's security team to keep a watchful eye. Surveillance cameras and security patrols

Opposite: Waving and smiling for the press and public was a skill Prince William had practised since childhood

ensured that the farmhouse would be the safest student digs in the area! It also provided William and Kate with the ideal location to conduct their relationship away from the gossip mongers and the camera lenses.

From Balgove House William and Kate were able to set off at weekends in William's black VW Golf either for a long drive down to Highgrove House or for the shorter trip up to Birkhall on the Balmoral Estate. The general public was, as yet, unaware of the royal romance, but that was all set to change when the couple flew out in March 2004 for a skiing break with friends, and Prince Charles, at the royals' traditional ski retreat of Klosters in Switzerland. It was there, after having enjoyed lunch with friends, that William and Kate were captured on camera sneaking a hug and a tender kiss before returning to the slopes. Their secret was well and truly out.

William and Kate were now seen together at parties, including the 2004 Kate Kennedy Club charity ball. Once their exams were over they flew out to Mauritius to spend a holiday on the idyllic island of Rodrigues with a group of friends. When they returned, William had further holiday trips to America and a Mediterranean cruise to enjoy without the pleasure of Kate's company. Inevitably, the press began to suggest that the Royal Romance had bitten the dust but no such announcement was ever made by the couple themselves.

Unlike any ordinary couple, who would be expected to attend the weddings of friends or relations together, Kate was absent from some society weddings to which the young prince had been invited. Protocol undoubtedly prevented her attending some events: she was not, after all, as yet a member of the Royal Family. That did not stop William from bringing her along to the Prince of Wales's stag event in Klosters prior to his marriage to Camilla Parker-Bowles in April 2005. Again, protocol prevented Kate from attending the wedding, but her closeness with Prince William, and Prince Charles's fondness for Kate, were clear from the relaxed scenes in the Swiss mountains.

Opposite: A tender moment between William and Kate on the ski slopes of Zermatt in Switzerland following lunch in the sunshine with friends

Following pages: William and Kate receive their degrees from St Andrews University in June 2005

Kate did, however, attend the wedding of Hugh Van Cutsem and Rose Astor with William in June, although she walked into the beautiful old church in Burford in the Cotswalds alone – but only because William was one of the ushers.

William and Kate graduated just weeks after Prince Charles's wedding and, although the young couple entered the Younger Hall together for the graduation ceremony, they were obliged by custom to sit several rows apart. Afterwards, William went walkabout outside the hall, shaking hands with members of the public who had gathered to congratulate him and to catch a glimpse of The Queen, Prince Philip and Prince Charles, all of whom were present for the event. Kate's family, of course, had been there, too, but while William rushed to his girlfriend's side after the ceremony as soon as he could, this was not the proper time and place for the other members of their families to mingle.

Following the Graduation Ball at St Andrews and a round of parties in London, William flew out to New Zealand where he was to represent the Queen at official ceremonies marking the sixtieth anniversary of the end of the Second World War. He also had time to watch the touring British Lions rugby team lose to the mighty All Blacks before jetting off to Kenya where Kate and a select band of friends joined him at Lewa Wilderness Trails: luxury cottages on an estate run by the Craig family. Jecca Craig had at one time been identified as a front runner in the 'Prince William Marriage Stakes' and William had spent time on her family's estate in Kenya during his gap year. He learned about conservation, part of the estate having been turned into a wildlife sanctuary, and his stay there with Kate and their friends was also something of a working holiday for him. There was also plenty of time, however, for William and Kate to spend time together in the romantic setting of the African wilderness.

 Back in the UK, the couple had some serious thinking to do about their future careers. William had a series of royal duties lined up to keep him busy in the meantime and he knew that he would be heading for the Royal Military Academy Sandhurst

Opposite clockwise from top left: Kate arrives for the wedding of Hugh Van Cutsem and Rose Astor; Kate in relaxed mood; Kate and her sister, Pippa, with William about to take part in the Eton Old Boys 'Wall Game' in 2006; William at his Sandhurst passing out parade, 2006

before too long. William's duties involved work experience on the Chatsworth estate where he learned about land management and also worked behind the scenes as a butcher. He then had a spell working with financiers in the City of London and later trained with Mountain Rescue teams at RAF Valley in Anglesey, North Wales.

As patron of the homeless charity Centrepoint, he made a number of visits to learn about the charity projects and also took an interest in the community work of The Football Association. In the meantime, he passed his Regular Commissions Board and was scheduled to begin training to become an army officer at Sandhurst in January 2006.

Kate, on the other hand, had yet to decide on a career path. She did not have the royals' 'family business' to keep her busy, and was drafted into her parents' company, Party Pieces, to work on their website and on catalogue material. She also took on part-time work as a buyer for the clothing company Jigsaw Junior, under an arrangement that was flexible enough to allow her to be with William whenever he was free from his training at Sandhurst. In December 2006, Kate was present at William's passing out parade when he was commissioned as a second lieutenant in the Blues and Royals, just as his brother, Prince Harry, had been earlier in the year.

It was a testing time for the couple. William now had to become more involved in army life, undertaking his tank commander's course and balancing his army duties with his royal duties. Kate had to endure constant press attention and found it increasingly difficult even to walk along the street without a camera lens being shoved in her face. Most of this she had to cope with entirely on her own: because she was Prince William's girlfriend rather than his fiancée, the royal protection officers were only on hand when William was around.

The tensions put such a strain on their relationship that, around Easter 2007, they decided to go their separate ways.

Opposite: Kate moving back to her parents' house to escape the attentions of the press following her split with William

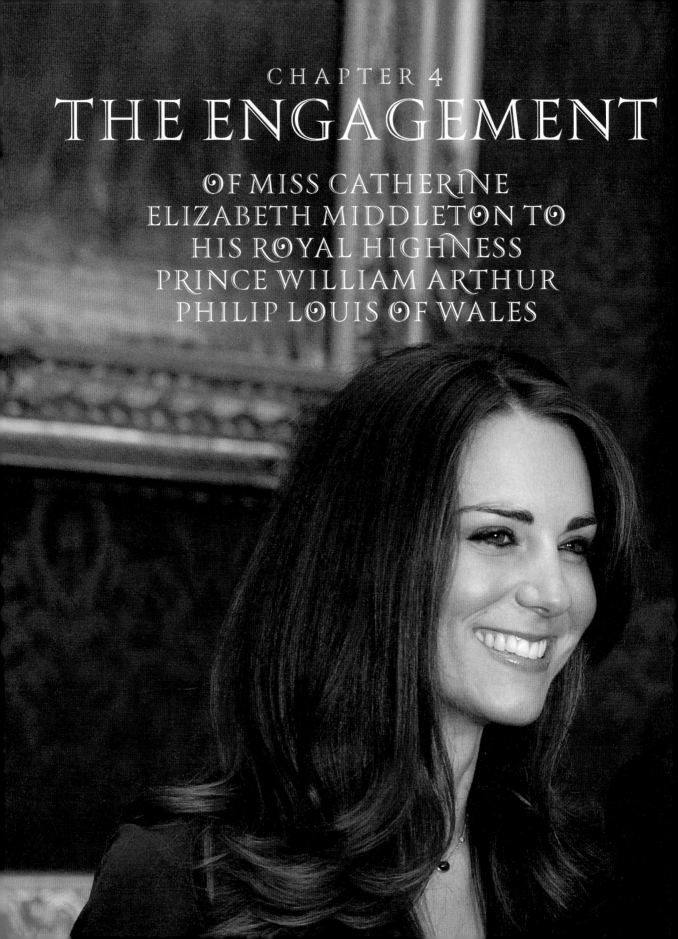

CHAPTER 4
THE ENGAGEMENT

OF MISS CATHERINE ELIZABETH MIDDLETON TO HIS ROYAL HIGHNESS PRINCE WILLIAM ARTHUR PHILIP LOUIS OF WALES

They say that breaking up is hard is hard to do – in fact, that's exactly how Neil Sedaka put it in his hit song twenty years before either Kate or William were even born. The classic love song captures the anguish of a relationship falling apart and, while so many people can relate to Sedaka's sentimental lyrics, far fewer people have had to go through the agony of parting while also knowing their misfortune would be discussed in bars, coffee shops and over dinner tables around the world.

Although he had his own feelings to deal with, William at least had some protection from attention outside whenever he decided he needed it, with either the royal household or the army to keep the press and public at bay. Kate, on the other hand, had no such barriers to hide behind. She retreated to her parents' home in Berkshire to wait for the fuss to die down.

There was inevitable speculation in the press about the causes of the breakdown of the couple's relationship, and as many expressions of sympathy. William and Kate had, after all, been a highly photogenic 'golden couple' who could be relied upon to brighten up the newspaper columns amid the bleak and dismal news on other fronts. There were also disparaging comments about how those who were closest to the throne might be best advised to look for romance among 'their own kind'. Commoners, some said, didn't really have the breeding for life in the royal spotlight and the strain would always tell eventually. When Princess Anne married Mark Phillips, he had been a commoner, and their marriage ended in divorce. When Prince Charles married Lady Diana Spencer, she was also technically a commoner, as was Sarah Ferguson when she married Prince Andrew, and those marriages also ended in disaster. But anyone who thought like that should have looked back another couple of generations to King George VI. While he was still Prince Albert and had no notion of becoming king, he married Lady Elizabeth Bowes-Lyons who was, like Diana, technically a commoner in that she had no royal title. Together they led the country through

Opposite clockwise from top left: William at the Cenotaph for Remembrance Day, 2009; with his father and Camilla at the commemoration service to mark the end of hostilities in Iraq, 2009; laying a wreath at the Cenotaph for Remembrance Day, 2009; at the Manchester Aquatic Centre for the Women's European Nations Water Polo Championships

the dark years of the Second World War and devoted the rest of their lives to public service and their royal responsibilities. If the love is strong enough to hold true then being born with the right form of title really isn't an issue.

Army life for William over the next few months was interspersed with a scattering of royal duties and a few evenings out with friends at his favourite nightspots in London, although, naturally, he was not seen at what had been his usual haunts in the company of Kate. She steeled herself to step back in front of the camera lenses again, moving back to her parents' flat in London rather than the house in Berkshire and being seen out on the town in the company of her little sister, who had finished her finals at Edinburgh in May. Pippa had also broken up with her boyfriend and the sisters went out together. They attended cultural events such as the launch of author Simon Sebag Montefiore's book *Young Stalin*, but also hit the dance floors of their favourite exclusive clubs.

William and Harry hosted the Concert for Diana at Wembley Stadium on 1 July 2007, the day that would have been her forty-sixth birthday. Ten years after her death, her sons had decided to celebrate her life by staging a concert to raise money for charities with which she, and now they, were involved. The new stadium had opened only a couple of months previously and the concert was a huge event to be televised around the world. The list of performers included Diana's favourites Duran Duran, Sir Elton John, Sir Tom Jones, Bryan Ferry and Rod Stewart as well as some of the Princes' choices such as P Diddy, Joss Stone and Kanye West. There was an audience of 63,000, with millions of others tuning in and with such a spectacle few noticed that in the royal box, just a few seats away from William and Harry, Kate was singing and clapping along with the rest of the audience. The couple did nothing to suggest that they were, after three months, now back together, but they were, quite definitely, a couple once again.

The following month William and Kate holidayed together in the Seychelles on the island of Desroches, a sliver of tropical

Opposite clockwise from top left: Harry and William playing polo at Cirencester Park – but the camera's focus is on Kate; William and Kate arrive back at Heathrow following a holiday in Scotland in 2009; William dressed for polo action at Cirencester Park in June 2009

Defence Helicopter Flying School

Search And Rescue Training Unit

paradise nestling serenely in the Indian Ocean. On this occasion, there was no posse of friends in tow and the couple strolled on the white-sand beaches, sunbathed and relaxed. Undoubtedly they realised this would be the calm before the storm. When they returned to the UK they would once again be the centre of media attention while William had a testing time ahead of him in the military.

As the future head of Britain's armed forces, William knew that, while Harry could dedicate his service life to the army, he had to have experience of all branches of the military. He had also expressed a desire, like Harry, to see active service, although this had so far been officially denied him. William was released on secondment from the Blues and Royals to the RAF where, having passed the flight-crew tests, he underwent an intensive training course to be presented with his wings by his father at RAF Cranwell in April 2008. A very proud Kate was there to witness the ceremony. Only later did the world learn that, while training with the RAF, he had been part of the crew of a giant C-17 Globemaster jet transport that had been on a mission to Afghanistan.

The navy then had its turn at showing their future commander-in-chief what their version of military life was all about. William trained with the Royal Navy for two months over the summer of 2008, on warships and submarines, with the Fleet Air Arm and with the Royal Marines. He then joined HMS *Iron Duke* for a five-week deployment to the Caribbean, taking part in various operations including the seizure of a boat being used to smuggle £40 million worth of cocaine.

Having originally signed on for a three-year short-service commission, it was expected that William's military career would soon draw to a close, but in the autumn of 2008 it was announced that he would be extending his commisson and, in fact, transfer from the Blues and Royals to the RAF. William's training as a helicopter pilot then began in earnest. With his father, his uncle Andrew and his brother all qualified to fly helicopters, William undoubtedly felt pressurised to do well, but he also knew that

Opposite top: William with Kate at his RAF wings graduation ceremony, April 2008

Opposite bottom: The sign outside William's future base at RAF Valley

this was his only route to real operational activity within the armed forces. The second-in-line to the throne would not be permitted to lead a reconnaissance force of Scimitar tanks into action with the Blues and Royals and William knew he would be sidelined to a non-operational role in the Royal Navy, so he set his heart on becoming a pilot with the RAF's Search and Rescue Force, a vital division he had seen at first hand when training with the Mountain Rescue Teams in North Wales shortly after leaving university.

Helicopter pilot training involves navigational exercises that range over hundreds of miles and William came in for some criticism when he organised some of his flights in an RAF Chinook to buzz his father's home at Highgrove, land (but not get out of the aircraft) in the grounds of Kate's parents' house and overfly his grandmother's house at Sandringham in Norfolk. All of these little adventures were described by the RAF as being perfectly normal training exercises. Pilots, after all, must be able to plot a course and follow the route. They also have to be able to land in places other than regular RAF bases. All of the correct permissions had been obtained and procedures followed for William's exercises. The press and public, of course, were sceptical. It sounded as if the Prince were being given carte blanche to use a £10 million helicopter for a bit of a lark. They may have had a point when an exercise apparently intended to test navigational skills, especially while flying over open water, resulted in William using a helicopter to pick up his brother from Woolwich Barracks in London before flying to RAF Bembridge in the Isle of Wight. On the island they attended their cousin, Peter Phillips' stag party.

While her boyfriend learned how to become a helicopter pilot with the RAF, Kate went about her business, working for her parents and for Jigsaw, keeping herself busy, although, unlike other young women hurrying to get to work in the morning, she had to put a bit of thought into what she wore. She had been voted one of the world's top-ten best-dressed women by *Tatler* magazine – surely something of a feather in the cap of someone who did, after all,

Opposite top: William about to take to the air in a Bell Griffin helicopter

Opposite bottom: Fixed wing training in a Hawk jet

Following pages: William and Kate on a return visit to St Andrews in 2011; at New Zealand House in London to sign the book of condolence for the earthquake victims

work as a fashion buyer, and the fashion industry began to experience what they dubbed 'The Middleton Effect': whenever Kate was seen on the arm of Prince William, whatever she was wearing was examined in great detail and then, within a matter of days –sometimes hours – it sold out of stores all over the country.

There was one accessory, however, that no one would really have wanted to copy. Prince William was reported to have given Kate a pair of antique pearl earrings for her twenty-eighth birthday, a gift with which Kate was duly thrilled. Unfortunately, after wearing them one evening she took them off and left them on her bedside table. When she woke she was horrified to find that they were missing. She was even more upset to find her pet spaniel, Otto, sitting on her bed looking at her with big, brown, guilty spaniel eyes. He'd thought the earrings were some kind of treat and had eaten them!

William suggested that Kate take Otto for a walk and . . . see what transpired. Eventually, the treasured earrings did reappear but they had been so badly chewed that, even when fastidiously cleaned, they were clearly ruined. William, it is said, simply promised Kate that he would replace them. Otto was not available for comment.

On 17 September 2010, Prince William graduated from his course at the Search and Rescue Training Unit at RAF Valley in Anglesey as a qualified SAR Sea King pilot. He was assigned to No 22 Squadron, initially as a co-pilot, and is expected to spend a three-year tour of duty with the squadron at RAF Valley. Two weeks later, William flew in a four-man Sea King crew when they were called out by Liverpool Coastguard. They picked up a man from an offshore gas rig in Morecambe Bay – he'd had a suspected heart attack and was delivered safely to hospital.

Later that month, William and Kate took a holiday in Africa, returning to Lewa in Kenya where, on 19 October, William asked Kate to marry him. He presented her with his mother's engagement ring. He had kept it hidden in his rucksack for three weeks until the moment he proposed and later described

Opposite: William is presented with his qualification certificate to become an operational Search and Rescue pilot flying RAF Sea King helicopters

Following pages: Kate training on the River Thames with 'The Sisterhood' team, although she had to pull out before the team's successful charity cross-channel race; Kate attempts to keep a low profile at Cirencester Park polo ground, 2009; tossing a pancake in Belfast on Shrove Tuesday, 2011

keeping the ring safe almost as nerve-racking as actually popping the question. The ring, he later said, was his way of keeping his mother involved in the wedding as she was not there to join in all of the fun and excitement. Kate simply described the proposal as 'very romantic', saying of her fiancé that 'There's a true romantic in there.' All of that, of course, came after the official announcement of the engagement on 16 November 2010. By then the date for the wedding – 29 April 2011 – had been pencilled in, although it would not be confirmed for some time. A great deal of organisation had to be arranged before then.

Westminster Abbey was the venue and if the happy couple had ever harboured any innocent preference for a quiet, intimate wedding day, those thoughts were immediately banished. Invitations were sent out to 1,900 guests including British and foreign royalty, celebrities, government officials, foreign dignitaries and friends and family of the happy couple.

Music for the service was provided by the Choir of Westminster Abbey and the Chapel Royal Choir accompanied by the London Chamber Orchestra and the Fanfare Team from the Central Band of the Royal Air Force as well as the eight-man Fanfare Team of the State Trumpeters of the Household Cavalry.

After the ceremony, the bridal party rode in coaches along the processional route to a reception at Buckingham Palace hosted by The Queen. They and their 600 guests were serenaded by Claire Jones, official harpist to The Prince of Wales. Following the afternoon reception, 300 guests stayed on for dinner and dancing at the evening reception.

It had been the wedding of the century.

Opposite: Practising for signing the register on the big day? Actually, they are signing the book of condolence for the victims of the New Zealand earthquake

Following pages: William and Kate at Trearddur Bay Lifeboat Station in Anglesey in February 2011, launching a new Atlantic 85 Inshore Lifeboat; the official engagement photocall, November 16, 2010

CHAPTER 5
THE MARRIAGE

OF HER ROYAL HIGHNESS
THE PRINCESS ELIZABETH
& HIS ROYAL HIGHNESS
THE DUKE OF EDINBURGH
20 NOVEMBER 1947

The Queen and the Duke of Edinburgh celebrated their diamond wedding in 2007. Their wedding ceremony in Westminster Abbey in November 1947 had been recorded by the BBC and broadcast to around 200 million radio listeners around the world. Television broadcasting had recently restarted after its suspension during the Second World War and viewers lucky enough to be able to crowd around a TV set saw the happy couple leave the Abbey in a carriage riding through streets thronging with wellwishers. It was a momentous and uplifting event for a population recovering from a most devastating war and struggling to survive with basic foodstuffs still either rationed or in short supply. The Queen, then Princess Elizabeth, needed ration coupons to buy the material for her wedding dress.

Her husband was the dashing young naval officer. Prince Philip of Greece and Denmark, who must have seemed remarkably grown up to the young Princess Elizabeth when she first met him: he had been thirteen years old and she only eight. The occasion was the marriage of Philip's cousin, Princess Marina of Greece and Denmark, to Elizabeth's uncle, the Duke of Kent, in 1934. Prince Philip and Princess Elizabeth were distant cousins, and met infrequently over the next few years as Philip attended schools in Germany and then in Scotland at Gordonstoun.

It was after he left Gordonstoun and joined the Royal Navy that Philip became re-acquainted with the then thirteen-year-old Princess Elizabeth when King George VI and Queen Elizabeth visited Dartmouth Naval College. Philip, still only a teenager himself, was asked to escort Princess Elizabeth and her younger sister, Princess Margaret. Philip and Elizabeth kept in touch by letter as he continued his studies, graduating from the college as the top cadet on his course in 1940. By this time, of course, Britain was at war.

Philip was commissioned as a midshipman and served at first in the Far East, before transferring to the Mediterranean Fleet and the battleship HMS *Valiant*. He saw action during the Battle of Crete and was mentioned in despatches for his bravery during

Opposite top: The wedding party at Buckingham Palace including King George VI and Queen Elizabeth

Opposite bottom: On the balcony at Buckingham Palace, left to right, King George VI, the bridesmaids, Princess Elizabeth, the Duke of Edinburgh, Queen Elizabeth and Queen Mary

the Battle of Cape Matapan in late March 1941. After another spell ashore completing training courses, Philip was promoted to sub-lieutenant and saw further active service on convoy duty before being promoted to first lieutenant of HMS *Warspite* when he was still only twenty-one years old, making him the navy's youngest first lieutenant. Posted to the Far East again, Philip watched the Japanese surrender aboard the USS *Missouri* in Tokyo Bay in 1945.

Princess Elizabeth had also been in uniform during the war years, when she joined the Women's Auxiliary Territorial Service in February 1945. She learned how to drive and service military trucks and is today the only living head of state who served in uniform during the Second World War.

The young couple became engaged in 1946 when Philip formally asked King George VI for his daughter's hand, but The King insisted they wait until Elizabeth's twenty-first birthday before they made an official announcement. Princess Elizabeth was in Kenya on a royal tour with her parents when she celebrated her birthday in April 1947, so the engagement was announced in July.

Several problems had to be overcome before the couple could actually marry. Prince Philip had to renounce his Greek and Danish titles and swear allegiance to the British crown, although that was no great problem for an officer serving in His Majesty's Royal Navy. As a result, he became Lieutenant Philip Mountbatten, taking his surname from his mother's family connections.

Philip had to convert from the Greek Orthodox religion to become an Anglican and to adopt Britain as his permanent home by becoming a naturalised British subject. He also had to have a new title. Princess Elizabeth would be expected to take her husband's name when they married and Philip, therefore, had to be suitably ennobled. Immediately before the wedding, King George VI proclaimed that Philip should be known as His Royal Highness, and he was awarded the titles Duke of

Opposite: Following the announcement of their engagement, Princess Elizabeth and Lieutenant Mountbatten appeared on the balcony at Buckingham Palace with the king, the queen and Princess Margaret to acknowledge the thousands who had gathered outside the palace gates

Edinburgh, Earl of Merioneth and Baron Greenwich of Greenwich in the County of London. When they were married, Princess Elizabeth would become the Duchess of Edinburgh.

The wrangling over the guest list at any wedding is the thing that causes most tension between the families of the bride and the groom, but there were some especially awkward and delicate issues to be tackled for Elizabeth and Philip's marriage. Philip's family had strong German connections, as did the British Royal Family, and his three sisters had married German princes before the war which had ended only two years before. Throughout Britain, feelings were still running high against the Germans, so certain relatives were not to be invited. Regardless, the list eventually ran to 2,000 guests.

The night before the wedding, Philip enjoyed two stag parties, one at the Dorchester Hotel in London, where the press were invited to take photographs, and another at the Belfry Club, an establishment now run by star chef Anton Mosimann.

On the day, Princess Elizabeth had eight bridesmaids, including her sister, Margaret. The others were her three cousins, Princess Alexandra of Kent, The Hon. Margaret Elphinstone and The Hon. Diana Bowes-Lyon; Lady Caroline Montagu-Douglas-Scott; Lady Mary Cambridge; Lady Elizabeth Lambart; and Philip's cousin, The Hon. Pamela Mountbatten. The page boys were Elizabeth's cousins Prince William of Gloucester and Prince Michael of Kent.

On the big day, the Duke of Edinburgh set out for Westminster Abbey with his best man, the Marquess of Milford Haven. Princess Elizabeth then arrived in the Irish State Coach, accompanied by her father, King George VI.

The princess's wedding dress was designed by Sir Norman Hartnell and was made from silk that had come from Chinese silk worms at Lullingstone Castle and woven in Dunfermline in Scotland. Her wedding ring was made of Welsh gold from the Clogau St David's mine.

Thousands of people lined the processional route from the

Previous spread: The official wedding photograph of the happy couple with the best man, bridesmaids and page boys

Opposite top: Lieutenant Mountbatten had two stag parties, one at the Dorchester and one at the Belfry Club

Opposite bottom: Bridesmaids Princess Margaret and Princess Alexandra of Kent on their way to the wedding

Following pages: The Duke and Duchess of Edinburgh in slightly more relaxed wedding portraits

Abbey to Buckingham Palace, where a wedding breakfast was held in the Ball Supper-room.

The wedding cake, made by McVities & Price, was in four tiers and stood nine feet (2.74m) high. The Duke of Edinburgh's sword, itself a wedding present from The King, was used to cut the official cake, although eleven other cakes had been received as wedding presents. Pieces of cake and food parcels were later distributed to schoolchildren across the country.

Reading out the wedding telegrams was traditionally the best man's job, but the Marquess would have struggled with that task as more than 10,000 had been received. There were also 2,500 wedding presents, ranging from two pairs of bed socks sent by a member of the public to a gold-and-jade necklace from Egypt's King Farouk.

The happy couple travelled from Waterloo station, along with Elizabeth's corgi, Susan, to spend their wedding night at the home of Philip's uncle, Earl Mountbatten, in Hampshire and travelled on from there to spend their honeymoon on the Balmoral Estate in Scotland.

Opposite top: Princess Elizabeth waves to the crowds as she returns to Buckingham Palace with her new husband

Opposite bottom: On the balcony at Buckingham Palace, left to right, King George VI, Princess Margaret, Lady Mary Cambridge, Princess Elizabeth, the Duke of Edinburgh, Queen Elizabeth and Queen Mary

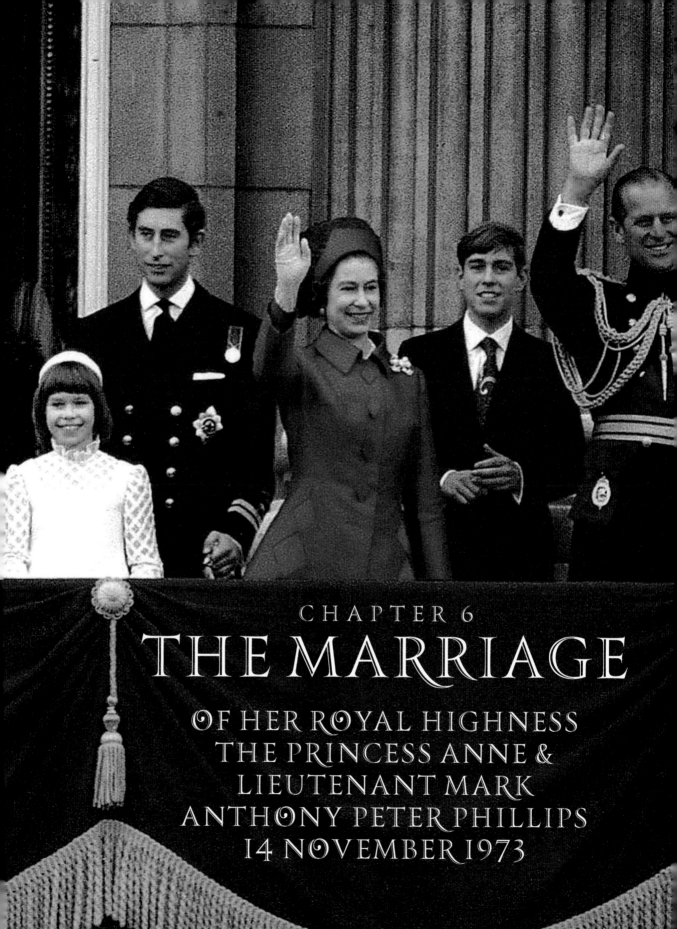

CHAPTER 6
THE MARRIAGE
OF HER ROYAL HIGHNESS THE PRINCESS ANNE & LIEUTENANT MARK ANTHONY PETER PHILLIPS 14 NOVEMBER 1973

The Queen's only daughter was born in 1950 in Clarence House, the London home of the Queen (then still Princess Elizabeth, Duchess of Edinburgh) and the Duke of Edinburgh. Princess Elizabeth and her husband had leased a home near Windsor Castle after their marriage in 1947 and had lived for a time in Malta when the Duke was stationed there with the Royal Navy. Clarence house was given to them in 1949. During the war it had been used as the headquarters for the Red Cross and the St John Ambulance Brigade and prior to that it had been the royal residence of Queen Victoria's third son, Prince Arthur, until his death in 1942. The young family, including, of course, Prince Charles who was by then a toddler, were not to live at Clarence house for long. In February 1952, King George VI, whose health had been failing, died while Princess Elizabeth and the Duke of Edinburgh were in Kenya on a tour that had also been scheduled to take in Australia and New Zealand. Although her coronation would not take place until June the following year, Princess Elizabeth returned to London as Queen and the family moved into Buckingham Palace.

It was in Buckingham Palace that Princess Anne Elizabeth Alice Louise began her education under the tutelage of a governess, Catherine Peebles, just as her older brother had done. To allow the young princess to mix with girls of her own age, the 1st Buckingham Palace Company Girl Guides was reformed in 1959. The company had been disbanded some years before, having first been formed so that The Queen, then Princess Elizabeth, could become a Girl Guide in 1937. The company was generally made up of children from the royal household and palace employees.

When she was thirteen, Princess Anne was sent to a boarding school, Benendon School in Kent, where she spent five years and left with six O levels and two A levels. By this time she was also passionate about horse riding and trained at the famous Spanish Riding School in Vienna.

When she was twenty-one, Princess Anne became European Eventing Champion and was voted BBC Sports Personality of the

Opposite clockwise from the top: Princess Anne and Lieutenant Mark Phillips on their way to Buckingham Palace in May 1973, their engagement having been announced the evening before; chefs from the Army School of Catering putting the finishing touches to the wedding cake; posing in the grounds of Buckingham Palace for the official engagement photo call

Year in 1971. In 1976 she competed as part of the British equestrian team at the Olympic Games in Montreal.

It was through their shared love of horses that Princess Anne met the young cavalry officer Lieutenant Mark Phillips. Born in 1948, Phillips was the son of Major Peter Phillips and Patricia Phillips. He attended Stouts Hill Prep School near the village of Uley in the Cotswalds (the school has now been turned into timeshare holiday properties) and Marlborough College, before entering the Royal Military Academy Sandhurst. He was commissioned as a second lieutenant in the Queen's Dragoon Guards in 1969, becoming a lieutenant, as is customary, in 1971 after two years' service.

An expert horseman, Phillips won the Badminton Horse Trials in 1971, 1972, 1974 and 1981. In 1972, he competed as part of the British three-day event team that won the gold medal at the Olympic Games in Munich.

The engagement of Princess Anne to Lieutenant Phillips was announced on 29 May 1973 and their wedding took place on 14 November of the same year at Westminster Abbey. The Princess wore a tudor-style silk dress embroidered with pearls around the high neck and across the shoulders. The dress had wide, medieval 'trumpet' sleeves and was made by Maureen Baker, chief designer for Susan Small, although fifteen dressmakers actually worked on the gown, each being given a section to make and none knowing exactly how the finished item would turn out, such was the secrecy surrounding how the princess's finished dress would look!

Princess Anne had her cousin, Lady Sarah Armstrong-Jones, as a bridesmaid and her youngest brother, Prince Edward as a page boy. Lieutenant Phillips wore the scarlet-and-blue dress uniform of the Queen's Dragoon Guards. Their marriage ceremony was broadcast on television worldwide, with estimates of the global audience ranging from 100 million upwards.

From Westminster Abbey, the happy couple rode in a carriage along a processional route to Buckingham Palace where they

Opposite clockwise from top left: During the ceremony at Westminster Abbey; Princess Anne presents her bouquet to Lady Sarah Armstrong-Jones as she leaves the abbey; the happy couple arriving at Buckingham Palace after the ceremony; waving to the crowds on the balcony at the palace with Prince Edward and Lady Sarah Armstrong-Jones

Following pages: The Queen and the Duke of Edinburgh returning to Buckingham Palace after the ceremony

appeared on the balcony to wave to the cheering crowds. The following day the couple boarded a flight at Heathrow to fly out to the West Indies where they honeymooned aboard the Royal Yacht Britannia. Lieutenant Phillips became Captain Phillips and was appointed a Personal Aide-de-Camp to Her Majesty The Queen, who also bought Princess Anne and her husband a country estate at Gatcombe Park in Gloucestershire, just a few miles from Prince Charles's country home, Highgrove House.

The couple were to have two children, Peter (born in 1977), and Zara (born in 1981) but the marriage was in trouble by the late eighties and in 1989 Princess Anne and Captain Phillips decided to separate. They divorced in April 1992.

In December 1992, Princess Anne married for a second time. Her husband, Commander Timothy Laurence was a former Equerry to The Queen. Because Princess Anne had been divorced, they could not marry in the Church of England but did so instead at the Church of Scotland's Crathie Kirk traditionally attended by the Royal Family when they are in residence at the nearby Balmoral Castle. In stark contrast to Princess Anne's first wedding in Westminster Abbey, only thirty family members and friends were in attendance at Crathie Kirk. Princess Anne and Commander Laurence had insisted on a low-key affair, although 300 local wellwishers came along to cheer the couple as they left the church.

While Princess Anne continued to be one of the hardest-working royals, deeply involved in a variety of charities and with a diary overloaded with more engagements than any other member of her family, Commander Laurence pursued a successful naval career. He was a staff officer with the Ministry of Defence and when promoted to captain in 1995, he returned to sea in command of the frigate HMS *Cumberland*. He is now a Vice-Admiral.

Opposite clockwise from top left: Princess Anne and Lieutenant Phillips set off on their honeymoon; waving to the crowds as they leave Buckingham Palace; en route to Heathrow to fly out to the West Indies to join the Royal Yacht Britannia; Princess Anne leaves her second wedding driven by her husband, Commander Tim Laurence and with her children, Peter and Zara, also in the car; Prince Charles, his parents and his grandmother leave his sister's wedding in 1992

Following spread: Traditional balcony scenes at Princess Anne's first wedding in 1973

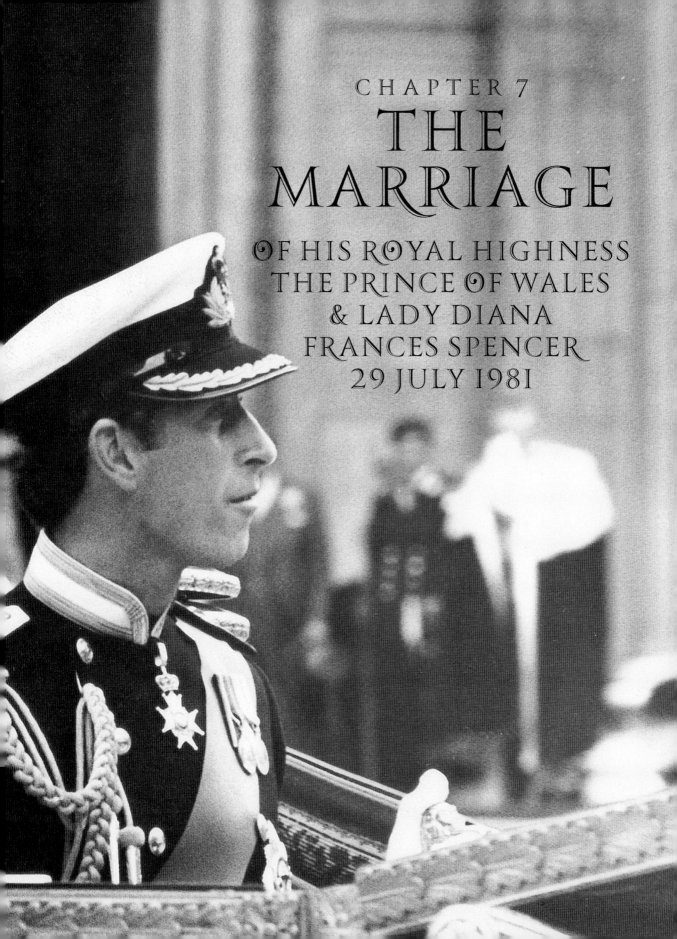

CHAPTER 7
THE MARRIAGE
OF HIS ROYAL HIGHNESS THE PRINCE OF WALES & LADY DIANA FRANCES SPENCER
29 JULY 1981

From the very beginning the marriage of Prince Charles, the heir to the throne and known as one of the world's most eligible bachelors, and Lady Diana, a beautiful young English rose whom people revered as Charles's 'fairytale princess', was referred to as 'the wedding of the century'. That, of course, was last century. More recently the term has been used to refer to the wedding of their son, Prince William. It is easy to draw comparisons, not least with the fact that both men are destined one day to be king.

In the eyes of the public and in society chatter, Prince Charles's name had been linked to a number of young ladies who were seen as potential brides. Lady Diana Spencer, however, was something of an unknown quantity when the glare of public attention first fell upon her. Diana was born at Park House near the village of Sandringham in Norfolk which, of course, has royal connections through Sandringham House, a Victorian country house built by Queen Victoria's son Prince Edward, Prince of Wales, on the site of a previous hall that had been bought for him by his mother but which was ultimately deemed too small. Sandringham House and the Sandringham Estate have remained in the possession of the Royal Family ever since and are used as a holiday retreat.

Born in July 1961, Diana was the third daughter of Edward John Spencer, Viscount Althorp, and the Honourable Frances Ruth Roche. Through her parents she had a number of royal connections. She was descended on her father's side, through illegitimate lines, from King Charles II and on her mother's side, again through illegitimate ties, to King James II. Naturally, there are many thousands of people who can claim such links to royalty in the distant past, but Diana's family had a far more direct link to the British throne through her maternal grandmother, Lady Fermoy, who had been a close confidante and lady-in-waiting to the Queen Mother. Furthemore, Diana's father had been equerry to King George VI and also to Queen Elizabeth II. Lady Diana's royal credentials, both past and present, were of the highest order outside of the current Royal Family itself.

Opposite: Lady Diana Spencer was young, slightly naïve and not at all well prepared to be thrust into the royal spotlight

Diana began her education at Silfield School in Kings Lynn, Norfolk before moving to Riddlesworth Hall boarding school, also in Norfolk, and then the exclusive West Heath Girls' School in Sevenoaks, Kent, a boarding school where she and her two sisters, Sarah and Jane, were among only 100 pupils. Despite her expensive education, Diana was not academically inclined, although she had an ear for music and was a good pianist. On leaving West Heath, Diana spent some time at the Institut Alpin Videmanette, a finishing school in Switzerland, before moving to London to live in her mother's flat.

For a short time, Diana lived with her mother in London (her parents had divorced when she was seven years old). Her father, however, had gained custody of his three daughters and their younger brother, Charles. With her mother spending most of her time in Scotland, Diana had to fend for herself in the flat but for her eighteenth birthday she was given her own flat in Earls Court. Diana enjoyed an anonymous lifestyle, and worked as a nanny and in a kindergarten. She would remain in obscurity for a little less than two years before becoming one of the most photographed young women in the world.

Prince Charles attended Hill House School in London, the first heir to the British throne ever to go to school (rather than receive private tuition), after being educated by his governess at Buckingham Palace, but was there for only ten months before moving to his father's old school, Cheam Preparatory School, in Hampshire, as a boarder. In 1958, while only a nine-year-old, Charles became Prince of Wales and Earl of Chester. In 1962, he was sent to another of his father's old schools, Gordonstoun in Scotland. Although he detested the harsh regime, he eventually was made head boy and enjoyed the two terms he spent as an exchange student at Timbertop, an outpost of the Geelong Church of England Grammar School in Melbourne, Australia.

In 1967, Charles left Gordonstoun with six O levels and two A levels, to study archaeology and anthropology at Trinity College, Cambridge. He later changed his courses and gained

Opposite: After her engagement to Prince Charles was announced, Diana became one of the most photographed young women in the world

a degree in history. While at Cambridge Charles also trained as a pilot with the RAF and on leaving university he continued his training at RAF Cranwell, flying jet aircraft. Following his passing out parade he attended the Royal Naval College at Dartmouth and served on the guided-missile destroyer HMS *Norfolk* as well as two frigates and, after qualifying as a helicopter pilot, on the commando carrier HMS *Hermes*. Prince Charles had his own command in the shape of the coastal minehunter HMS *Bronington* for his final nine months in the navy in 1976.

Charles had previously dated Diana's sister, Sarah, but it wasn't until Lady Diana watched him playing polo, when they were both guests at a weekend in the country, that they started to take an interest in each other. Charles invited Diana to join his party on a sailing weekend at Cowes in the Isle of Wight aboard the Royal Yacht *Britannia* and it was during a later stay at Balmoral that Diana was introduced to The Queen and Prince Philip. When Charles proposed during a private dinner at Buckingham Palace in February 1981, he asked Diana to keep her acceptance a secret until a formal announcement could be made. On 24 February 1981, when she was still only nineteen years old, Diana became officially engaged to The Prince of Wales, displaying an engagement ring consisting of a large sapphire nestling in a cluster of fourteen diamonds.

The wedding date was set for 29 July 1981 – four weeks after Diana's twentieth birthday – and the venue was to be St Paul's Cathedral.

St Paul's was chosen because it had more space for guests than Westminster Abbey, and more people would be able to watch the wedding procession as the coaches and their escorts wound their way through the streets of London from Buckingham Palace and Clarence House (from where Diana and her father would set off) to St Paul's. An estimated two million people lined the route. There were 4,000 police officers on duty to control the crowds along with 2,200 military personnel. Waiting in St Paul's Cathedral were 3,500 invited guests, while around the world a further 750 million watched the ceremony on television.

Opposite: Posing for the official engagement photographs, showing off the stunning sapphire and diamond ring and (middle right) Diana growing in confidence as she accompanies her fiancé on an official engagement

Diana arrived with her father at the cathedral in the Royal Glass Coach. She was wearing a £9,000 silk-taffeta wedding dress designed by David and Elizabeth Emanuel. The dress had a twenty-five foot long silk train and had been hand-embroidered with 10,000 mother-of-pearl sequins and pearls. In keeping with tradition, Diana wore something old – antique lace was incorporated into the dress design; something new – silk from Lullington in Dorset; something borrowed – a Spencer family tiara; and something blue – a small blue bow stitched into the waistband of the dress. For extra luck, the dress also had a little diamond-studded gold horseshoe sewn on. Although it looked light and puffy, the dress was actually quite heavy, especially considering that the bride was dragging yards of extra material behind her. Diana had to have special rehearsals to practice walking while wearing the dress.

Diana famously fluffed her lines when repeating Charles's name during the ceremony, saying 'Philip Charles Arthur George' instead of 'Charles Philip Arthur George', to which Prince Andrew reportedly quipped, 'She's just married my father!' Prince Andrew and Charles's youngest brother, Prince Edward, were Prince Charles's 'supporters', at the wedding (Royal weddings traditionally have one or more supporters instead of a best man).

Diana was attended by pageboys Lord Nicholas Windsor and Edward van Cutsem, both of whom were Prince Charles's godsons, and bridesmaids Lady Sarah Armstrong-Jones (Charles's cousin); India Hicks (granddaughter of Earl Mountbatten); Sarah-Jane Gaselee (great-granddaughter of Sir Winston Churchill) and Catherine Cameron (granddaughter of the Marquess of Lothian).

After the ceremony, The Prince and Princess of Wales set off for Buckingham Palace where they appeared on the balcony and, going against royal traditional, kissed in front of the cheering crowds. There were 120 guests at the palace for the wedding breakfast, although even they would have struggled to get through more than two dozen wedding cakes that had been given to the Prince and Princess. The official wedding cake had been made

Opposite: The Prince and Princess of Wales leaving Westminster Abbey as man and wife

Following pages: The procession through crowds of wellwishers on the way from the Abbey to Buckingham Palace

at the Royal Navy cookery school at HMS Pembroke (a shore station) in Chatham, Kent.

After the celebrations at the palace, Prince Charles and his bride left for Waterloo Station, just as his parents had done, to spend their wedding night at Broadlands, the Mountbatten family home in Hampshire. They then began a Mediterranean cruise, joining the Royal Yacht *Britannia* at Gibraltar and sailing to Algeria, Tunisia, Sicily, Egypt and the Greek islands before flying to Scotland, where they spent the final part of their three-month honeymoon at Balmoral.

Sadly, 'the wedding of the century' was not to bring about a lasting marriage, with Prince Charles and Princess Diana divorcing in 1996, well before the century was over. Tragically, Diana died in a horrendous car crash a year later.

On 9 April 2005, Prince Charles married again at a civil ceremony at the Guildhall in Windsor. Mrs Camilla Parker Bowles became his wife and took the title Her Royal Highness The Duchess of Cornwall. The Queen and Prince Philip were not present at the ceremony, but attended the blessing by the Archbishop of Canterbury in St George's Chapel in Windsor Castle. At the civil ceremony the couple's witnesses were Prince William and Camilla's son, Tom Parker Bowles. The Duchess and Prince Charles's wedding rings were made, as has become traditional, of 22-carat gold from the Clogau St David's mine in Wales.

Previous pages: Charles and Diana spent part of their honeymoon at Balmoral in Scotland; a kiss at a polo match; Diana, relaxed and confident as the Princess of Wales

Opposite clockwise from top left: Zara Phillips at the wedding of Prince Charles and Camilla in 2005; Tom Parker Bowles, Laura Parker Bowles and Princes Harry and William await the arrival of the bride and groom at the Guildhall in Windsor; Prince Charles and the Duchess of Cornwall after their civil ceremony, Prince Charles, Camilla and her son, Tom, at the Guildhall

CHAPTER 8

THE MARRIAGE

OF HIS ROYAL HIGHNESS
THE PRINCE ANDREW
DUKE OF YORK &
MISS SARAH MARGARET
FERGUSON
23 JULY 1986

Polo had always been a passion for Major Ronald Ferguson. A former officer in the Life Guards, one of the regiments of the Household Cavalry, Ferguson retired from the army in 1968, becoming heavily involved in polo thereafter, running Dummer Down, his family farm in Hampshire and acting as polo manager first to the Duke of Edinburgh (with whom he had played polo) and then to Prince Charles.

The Fergusons had age-old connections to Britain's senior aristocracy and the Royal Family, but it was through polo that Major Ferguson's younger daughter, Sarah, came to know her future husband. Not that either of them were hugely interested in the sport – they came to know each other as children chasing each other around on the sidelines while the grown-ups watched men chasing each other around on horseback.

Born in October 1959, Sarah is four months older than Andrew and was brought up on Dummer Down Farm. She was educated at boarding school and later attended secretarial college. Her mother, Susan, and her father separated when she was thirteen and Susan left to live in Argentina where she later married a polo player and established their own ranch breeding polo ponies.

Sarah had a number of jobs after leaving college, including working for a PR firm and in an art gallery and in 1985 she was invited to a party at Windsor Castle to celebrate the Royal Ascot Races, where she once again met her childhood playmate, Prince Andrew.

Andrew had, by this time, earned himself a reputation as a man of action. Born in the Belgian Suite of Buckingham Palace, he was the first child born to a reigning monarch in Britain since Queen Victoria had been on the throne. Educated at first by a governess in Buckingham Palace, Andrew was then sent to Heatherdown Prep School before going on, as his father and older brother had, to Gordonstoun in Scotland. He also spent six months as an exchange student at Lakefield College School in Ontario, Canada.

Andrew left school with english, history, economics and political science A levels and chose not to go to university, opting

Opposite top: Major Ronald Ferguson and his daughter, Sarah, leaving Claridge's Hotel after lunching there in March 1986

Opposite bottom: A few days later, Sarah is snapped in the street following the announcement of her engagement to Prince Andrew

instead to join the Royal Navy. He went through a variety of exams and interviews, including tests at the Aircrew Selection Centre at RAF Biggin Hill, before being accepted to train as a helicopter pilot. He began his career in earnest at the Britannia Royal Naval College in Dartmouth in 1979 and during the following year also undertook the All Arms Commando Course at the Royal Marines training centre in Lympestone.

After passing out from Dartmouth, Andrew learned to fly first the small Gazelle-model helicopter and later the Sea King, before being posted to serve aboard the aircraft carrier HMS *Invincible* in 1982.

Prince Andrew's arrival aboard *Invincible* coincided with the ship's departure for the South Atlantic as part of the Falklands armada. He saw active service with the Royal Navy Task Force as a Sea King co-pilot, flying as a missile decoy, on anti-submarine missions, on casualty evacuation and search-and-rescue flights. His commanding officer later described him as 'an excellent pilot'.

It was a seasoned veteran of the Falklands War, therefore, who Sarah Ferguson met at Windsor, and the two began seeing each other whenever Andew's ongoing commitment to his naval career would allow. A year later, at Floors Castle, the Duke of Roxburghe's country residence, where the couple had apparently shared their first kiss some time previously, Andrew asked Sarah to marry him.

The couple's official engagement was announced and they posed for the press in the gardens at Buckingham Palace on 19 March 1986. Sarah showed off an engagement ring consisting of an oval Burmese ruby (chosen by Andrew to match her flame-red hair) surrounded by a cluster of ten diamonds. Designed from a sketch that Andrew had done himself, the ring was made by Garrards of Regent Street and it was estimated at the time that such a ring would cost £25,000. The wedding date was set for 23 July, the venue to be Westminster Abbey.

Sarah wore a gown designed by Lindka Cierach and made of embroidered ivory silk with padded shoulders, a scooped

Opposite clockwise from top left: After she became engaged, Sarah was accompanied to work by a royal protection officer; Sarah arriving for the Easter service at St George's Chapel, Windsor Castle in 1986; official engagement photo of the ring Prince Andrew designed; the couple pose for an official engagement portrait; a kiss in the grounds of Buckingham Palace; a more relaxed pose in the palace gardens

neckline and beaded bumble bees on the bodice, the bumble bee featuring on Sarah's coat of arms. The dress also featured a seventeen-foot train and the veil appeared to be held on by a crown of flowers, although when the ceremony was over and Sarah had become Her Royal Highness, The Duchess of York (the Queen having created Andrew Duke of York, Earl of Inverness and Baron Killyleagh just before the wedding), the flowers were removed to reveal a tiara that had been leant to Sarah by her new mother-in-law.

Sarah had four bridesmaids, including her half-sister, Alice Ferguson, and Andrew's niece, Zara Phillips. There were also four page boys including Prince William and Zara's brother, Peter Phillips dressed in historic naval costumes.

From Westminster Abbey, the new Duke and Duchess rode in the State Landau to Buckingham Palace where they appeared on the balcony in front of an estimated 100,000 people. When the crowd called for them to kiss, as Andrew's older brother had done with Diana, the couple pretended not to hear until the crowd roared, at which point they obliged.

Following the wedding breakfast at Buckingham Palace, there was a further party at Claridges hotel in Mayfair for around 300 guests. The bride and groom then left for their honeymoon in the Azores.

On their return, they moved into Prince Andrew's apartments at Buckingham Palace and by the time their first child, Princess Beatrice Elizabeth Mary of York, was born, a twelve-bedroom mansion was under construction for them at Sunninghill Park in Berkshire. They moved into the house in 1990, around the time that their second daughter, Princess Eugenie Victoria Helena of York was born.

The marriage, however, was not built to last and six years after the wedding Sarah and Andrew separated, finally divorcing in May 1996.

Opposite clockwise from top left: Bridesmaid Alice Ferguson finds the ceremony a trifle tedious; Prince William gives a cheery wave as he rides in a carriage with his Uncle Edward; the Queen and Major Ferguson returning to the palace after the ceremony; the bride and groom acknowledge the crowds; the Queen Mother and Princess Margaret on their way to Buckingham Palace; the Duke of Edinburgh with Sarah's mother, Mrs Susan Barrantes

Following spread: The Duke and Duchess of York on their way to Buckingham Palace where they teased the crowd into cheering for the balcony kiss

CHAPTER 9
THE MARRIAGE

HIS ROYAL HIGHNESS
THE PRINCE EDWARD,
EARL OF WESSEX &
MISS SOPHIE HELEN
RHYS-JONES
19 JUNE 1999

It has been called 'the sport of kings', although most people nowadays associate that term with horse racing; it is also known as 'real tennis' or 'royal tennis'. It is a complex and skilful game that looks a bit like squash and a bit like lawn tennis but is actually a mystery to most people. Henry VIII loved it, as did Anne Boleyn, who was arrested while watching a game (and she complained bitterly because she had placed a bet and wanted to see the outcome!). Henry's real tennis court at Hampton Court is still in use today, Prince Edward being one of those who plays there. Edward is a big fan of the game, as he should be – it was through playing the sport that he met his future wife.

Prince Edward Anthony Richard Louis was born in Buckingham Palace on 10 March 1964, The Queen's fourth child and third son. He made his first public appearance that year at the Trooping of the Colour ceremony when The Queen brought him out on to the balcony at Buckingham Palace to show him off to the assembled crowds. Just as his older sister and brothers had been, Edward was educated at first by a governess at the palace. He then went to Gibbs School, a pre-prep school in Kensington until, in 1972, he was sent to Heatherdown Preparatory School near Ascot. Five years later, shadowing his father and older brothers, he went to Gordonstoun in Scotland. While there he played rugby, became a proficient skier and sailor, took gliding lessons and gained his Duke of Edinburgh's Gold Award. He was made Guardian, the Gordonstoun equivalent of Head Boy, in his final term and left the school with A-levels in History, English literature and Economic and Political Studies.

Before going on to university, Edward took time out in 1982 to teach English and History at Wanganui School in New Zealand where he also helped out with drama productions and lent a hand with Duke of Edinburgh's Award projects. Edward endured some controversy when he returned to England to take up a place at Cambridge University as his A-level results were not of the standard usually required for entry into their hallowed halls, but he threw himself into university life nonetheless, and took part

Opposite clockwise from top left: Sophie became the one every photographer wanted to snap after her engagement to Prince Edward was announced; being engaged to a prince also brought police protection; flowers of congratulation are carried from Sophie's office

in a number of stage productions. It was there that he learned to play real tennis. He graduated in 1986 with a 2:2 in History.

As is expected of young men in the Royal Family, Edward then proceeded to military service, training to become an officer in the Royal Marines. Eventually, however, he decided that the military life was not for him and resigned his commission in 1987, before he graduated. Rather than being a marine, Edward wanted to work in showbusiness. He worked for a couple of theatre companies, including Andrew Lloyd Webber's Really Useful Theatre Company and in 1993 he formed his own company, Ardent Productions. It was around this time that he met Sophie Rhys-Jones, a PR executive who had agreed to play at a charity real tennis match in place of tennis star and TV presenter Sue Barker.

Just nine months younger than Edward, Sophie was born at the Radcliffe Infirmary in Oxford in January 1965. While Sophie was still a little girl, her family moved to the picturesque village of Brenchley, near Tunbridge Wells in Kent. Sophie attended Dulwich College Preparatory School, Kent College School for Girls and West Kent College before deciding to pursue a career in public relations. She worked for a ski company in Switzerland and also worked in Australia and travelled for a year before returning to London and a job at Capital Radio. Sophie spent four years at Capital in the press department, moving on from there to work for PR companies The Quentin Bell Organisation and MacLaurin Communications & Media. It was while at MacLaurin that Sophie took part in the momentous real tennis match. Leaning playfully on Edward's shoulder during a post-match photo session, the lively blonde clearly caught the Prince's eye.

The couple's relationship developed from there, although both were keen still to pursue the careers on which they had embarked. Sophie established a PR partnership, RJH Public Relations in 1996 but, as Edward was also to find, it was difficult to pursue commercial interests while remaining close to the heart of the Royal Family.

On 6 January 1999 the engagement of Sophie and Prince Edward was announced. In a break from tradition, the wedding was not to

Opposite clockwise from top left: Sophie and Prince Edward on the balcony at Buckingham Palace to watch the Trooping of the Colour, 12 June 1999; Sophie and Edward are joined by the Queen Mother during the Trooping of the Colour ceremony; the three princes walk to St George's Chapel in Windsor for the wedding ceremony, 19 June 1999

take place at Westminster Abbey, the bride and groom having insisted on a low-key marriage ceremony. Instead, on 19 June 1999, they were married at St George's Chapel in Windsor Castle.

Sophie's dress was a long, fitted gown with long sleeves and an ivory train. Made from hand-dyed silk organza and silk crepe the ensemble incorporated rows of 325,000 pearls and crystal beading. She also wore a diamond tiara on loan from The Queen's private collection and a matching pearl necklace and earrings that were a gift from her husband. Edward eschewed the traditional uniform, as did his two brothers who acted as his supporters, and wore a morning suit. He carried in his pocket an 18-carat gold hunter watch that was a gift from Sophie. On the day of the wedding, The Queen conferred upon Prince Edward the titles Earl of Wessex and Viscount Severn, meaning that when he and Sophie were husband and wife she would become Her Royal Highness The Countess of Wessex.

Prince Charles, Prince Andrew and the groom walked to the chapel while the bride arrived in a limousine, although the newlyweds took a processional route in an open carriage to the wedding reception at Windsor Castle after the ceremony in order to acknowledge the crowds who had gathered to witness the occasion.

The 500 guests were mainly family and friends of the bride and groom and at the reception after the wedding breakfast they danced long into the night as the groom's erstwhile comrades in the Royal Marines Band played classic rock 'n' roll. The happy couple then set off by Rolls Royce for a night at the Queen Mother's Windsor residence, the Royal Lodge, before heading to their own new home at Bagshot Park a few miles south of Windsor. They then travelled north to Balmoral for a brief honeymoon prior to returning to work in London.

Unfortunately, accusations that they were using their royal status to drum up business, and difficult business conditions in a turbulent economic climate, led to the Earl and Countess withdrawing from commercial life to concentrate on royal duties and bringing up their children Lady Louise Windsor (born in 2003) and James, Viscount Severn (born in 2007).

Opposite clockwise from top left: Sophie arrives in style in one of the Queen's Rolls Royces; the bride is escorted up the chapel steps by her father, Christopher; waving to the assembled crowds on the route to Windsor Castle

CHAPTER 10

THE BEST MAN

HIS ROYAL HIGHNESS PRINCE HENRY CHARLES ALBERT DAVID OF WALES

Two years younger than Prince William, Prince Harry was, like his older brother, born in St Mary's Hospital in Paddington, London. He arrived on 15 September 1984 and within a few months he was off on his first royal trip, accompanying his parents to Italy. Princess Diana famously hated being separated from her sons and both boys began their globetrotting lifestyle while still babes in arms, despite Royal protocol demanding that, in case there were a tragic accident, the heir to the throne, the second in line and the third in line should not travel together on the same aircraft.

A lively and inquisitive child, Harry was often restless, pointing, asking questions and unable to remain still for long. He behaved, in other words, like any other child. His older brother, whose spirited nature had attracted a great deal of attention in the past, now tended to be less excitable by comparison, having had the benefit of two extra years of 'royal training'. Like William, Harry became a 'Little Cygnet' at Jane Mynors' Nursery School when he was three, then followed his older brother to Wetherby School two years later. The nursery and Wetherby were both in the Notting Hill area of London, just a stone's throw from Kensington Palace and the boys enjoyed spending their weeks in London and their weekends at Highgrove in the country. That all changed when Prince William was sent to Ludgrove School in Berkshire in 1990. With William attending boarding school, the brothers were separated for long periods for the first time and, although they undoubtedly missed each other, it did mean that Harry now had his mother's undivided attention – when she was around. Princess Diana's public life kept her incredibly busy, but she made strenuous efforts to arrange her engagements around her boys, even taking them to school herself whenever she could.

In 1992, Harry joined William at Ludgrove and they were together again for three years until William left for Eton. It was while Harry was looking forward to progressing to Eton himself that tragedy struck and Princess Diana was killed. In a black suit and tie, Harry walked behind his mother's funeral cortege along

Opposite clockwise from top left: At six months of age, Prince Harry arrives at Aberdeen airport for his first visit to Balmoral; Harry and William in the arms of their parents on a visit to Italy in 1985; Harry's first day at nursery school; the two princes at Wetherby School, 1989; on holiday with the Spanish royal family, 1987; Princess Diana takes her sons to school in 1988; a cuddle from Mum, Mallorca 1987

with his brother, his uncle (Diana's brother Earl Spencer), his father and his grandfather, Prince Philip. Harry paced the route that was lined by hundreds of thousands of weeping onlookers, bravely holding his composure. It was less than two weeks before his thirteenth birthday.

Harry passed the Eton entrance exams, moving to the Berkshire college in 1998. Like William, Harry enjoyed playing polo and rugby and broke his nose during one game in 2000. His association with both sports would continue long after he left school as he played polo regularly, even representing Young England when he was visiting Australia in 2003. He became heavily involved with rugby after training as a Development Officer with the Rugby Football Union in 2004. This led to him coaching and playing tag rugby with schoolchildren throughout England. He also played rugby with some of the orphans he visited in Lesotho in 2004 and in 2010 Harry was made vice patron of the Rugby Football Union, having previously been accorded the same honour by the Welsh Rugby Union in 2007. His grandmother, The Queen, is patron of both the RFU and WRU.

Harry's school days at Eton were marred by controversy over claims that he had received more help than was strictly permitted in order to complete his coursework to gain a B in art at A level and a D in geography. The uncomfortable storm of publicity was not the last that he would have to endure.

When he left Eton, Harry set off on a gap-year trip that took him to Australia, Argentina and Africa. Harry spent eight weeks in Lesotho in southern Africa, and made a documentary film about the hardships of the children he visited there who had been orphaned as a result of HIV/AIDS. Along with Prince Seeiso of Lesotho, he subsequently established a charity called Sentebale for the orphans. When the documentary was screened on TV at the end of 2004, it attracted donations of over £600,000 for Sentebale. In Sesotho, the language of Lesotho, Sentebale means 'forget me not.' Harry spends a great deal of time on fundraising efforts for Sentebale, including high-profile events such as charity polo

Opposite clockwise from top left: Learning to ski with brother, William, 1991; fun with Mum at Thorpe Park in 1993; following his mother's coffin in September 1997; showing his mother how to ride a jet ski in St Tropez in 1997

matches and, in 2008, a 1,000-mile, eight-day, off-road motorcycle trek across South Africa from Port Edward to Port Elizabeth. Prince William joined his brother for the epic motorcycle safari.

With his gap year over, Harry entered the Royal Military Academy Sandhurst in May 2005 where he successfully completed a forty-four-week course as an officer cadet. He was then commissioned as a 'Cornet' (Second Lieutenant) in the Blues and Royals, a regiment of the Household Cavalry. Harry trained as a tank commander in the Blues and Royals' Scimitar light tanks and was scheduled to be deployed with his unit to Iraq in May 2007. Because specific threats were made against his life, with one extremist group vowing to capture him whatever the cost, the army announced that it would be too dangerous for Harry to go. His presence, they decided, would put those around him in even greater danger than what they would normally expect. Harry appeared to accept the situation, even though he had allegedly been reported to threaten to resign his commission if he were not allowed to serve alongside the men he had trained with. Soldiers were said to have arrived in Iraq wearing T-shirts bearing a slogan that mimicked the famous scene from the film Spartacus (where a group of slaves all claim to be Spartacus in order to protect the eponymous hero), proclaiming 'I'm Harry!'

Harry was reported to have been sent on a training exercise in Canada and the issue of his deployment to the war zone fizzled out. The exercise in Canada, however, turned out to be preparation for deployment not to Iraq but to Afghanistan. Harry spent almost three months in secret, on the front line, calling in air strikes, patrolling hostile territory and helping Gurkha troops to fight off a Taliban attack. His cover was blown when the German and Australian press revealed that he was serving in the region and he had to be recalled.

In April 2008 Harry was promoted to lieutenant and within a few months began training as a helicopter pilot with the ultimate aim of flying Apache attack helicopters for the Army Air Corps. He and William went 'back to school' together, both training at

Opposite clockwise from top left: Meeting the Spice Girls with his father in South Africa in 1997; celebrating with England coach Clive Woodward after England won the Rugby World Cup in Sydney in 2003; polo at Cirencester in 2009; helping to build a school in Lesotho, South Africa in 2008; Remembrance Day service at the Cenotaph in 2009; Harry joins his family on the balcony at Buckingham Palace for the Battle of Britain Memorial Flight fly-past in 2005; preparing for the charity motorbike marathon across South Africa in 2008; always destined to be a soldier, here with the Light Dragoons in Germany in 1993

the Army Air Corps headquarters at Middle Wallop in Hampshire. Prince Charles, Colonel-in-Chief of the Army Air Corps, presented Harry with his wings at a ceremony in Middle Wallop on 7 May 2010.

Although his military training takes up most of his working life, Harry also performs a range of royal duties and is never very far from the news, not always for the best of reasons. When he was seventeen he was caught smoking cannabis and taking part in drinking binges at a pub near Highgrove. There have also been a few contretemps with photographers outside trendy nightclubs where both he and William enjoy spending time with their friends.

A number of girls have been linked to Harry but the most serious girlfriend he has had is Zimbabwean-born Chelsy Davy. The couple have had an on-off relationship since 2004 and Chelsy has accompanied Harry on various holiday trips, including skiing in Klosters. The prince remains, however, very much a bachelor even if one supposed company producing unofficial souvenirs to celebrate his brother's wedding saw things differently. The company apparently rushed a commemorative mug into production a little too quickly. The china mug was boldly pictured on the internet bearing the elaborate inscription 'A beautiful cup to commemorate the most beautiful occasion.' Above the inscription, in oval floral frames, as though two halves of the same romantic locket, were pictures of Kate and . . . Harry! It was later reported that the whole 'botched' job was a scam but such is the fervour created by the marriage of Harry's brother that even this silly joke made the news!

Opposite clockwise from top left: Prince Harry receives his Army Air Corps wings from his father, the regiment's Colonel-in-Chief, along with a trophy for showing the best tactical ability on his course; as Commodore-in-Chief of Small Ships and Diving, Prince Harry presents operational medals for service in Iraq to members of the Royal Navy's Mines Countermeasures Squadron; meeting girlfriend Chelsy Davy at Heathrow in 2007; Chelsy Davy at Royal Ascot in 2008; enjoying England versus France at Twickenham with Zara Phillips in 2011; clowning with children in Portsmouth; clowning with London city brokers in 2008

CHAPTER II
THE MAID OF HONOUR
PHILIPPA CHARLOTTE MIDDLETON

If a bride is going to have a Maid of Honour, or Senior Bridesmaid, then who better could it be than her sister? The Queen, after all, had her sister, Princess Margaret, as her Senior Bridesmaid, and if one future queen chose her sister, then there was surely no question that the next future queen would do the same. Of course, if a bride in those circumstances didn't choose her sister, then her sister might never speak to her again!

There was little chance of such a falling-out between the Middleton sisters. The two have been close ever since Philippa, known to everyone as 'Pippa', was born on 6 September 1983. With less than two years' age difference, the girls had always enjoyed shared interests and, just as Prince Harry followed his older brother through school, so too did Pippa follow Kate.

Before their education even began, however, the girls were whisked away to foreign parts when their father, Michael, was posted to Amman in Jordan. Michael worked for British Airways as a dispatcher, also known nowadays as an Airside Business Manager. The dispatcher is responsible for the aircraft up to the moment it leaves its stand, checking that it has the right amount of fuel, that it is not overloaded, that the flight crew is happy with the condition of the aircraft and co-ordinating the multitude of staff required to prepare a modern airliner for departure. If the dispatcher is not satisfied that the aircraft is safe and ready to leave, then it stays put.

Michael's father was a pilot instructor with British European Airways, which became British Airways when it merged with British Overseas Airways Corporation in 1974, and Michael had initially intended to train as a pilot, but found the job on the ground more to his liking. It was while working at Heathrow that Michael met Carole Goldsmith, a stewardess with British Airways. The two became an item and in 1979 they bought their first flat together, tying the knot officially in June 1980 when they married at a pretty little church in Buckinghamshire just half an hour's drive from their home in Slough.

Opposite top: Michael and Carole Middleton

Opposite bottom: Pippa joining in the fun at a friend's birthday party

Three years later, when Pippa came along, the young family was living in a modest house in Bradfield Southend in Berkshire. Pippa and her older sister became very much a part of the local community of children on their return from Jordan in September 1986, when their mother was expecting her third child, James, who was born in April 1987.

As if coping with three young children was not taxing enough, it was in 1987 that Carole decided to set up her own business. Having seen how so many young mums struggled when it came to organising their children's parties, Carole established Party Pieces, supplying everything required for a successful children's party by mail order – just add your own kids. With hard work and enthusiasm, Carole made such a success of the business that both she and Michael were soon involved full time, and when they launched a website, Party Pieces grew into a major concern. The company is now run from converted farm buildings in Ashampstead Common in Berkshire where they have a call centre in a 200-year-old barn and another converted barn 'stacked to the roof with literally hundreds and thousands of paper plates and party paraphernalia', according to their website.

It was the success of Party Pieces that allowed Michael and Carole to send both Kate and Pippa to Downe House boarding school and then to Marlborough College.

Having followed her older sister through school, Pippa also followed Kate north to university, although not as far as St Andrews. Pippa decided to study English at Edinburgh University. Pippa shared a flat in Edinburgh with some very eligible young bachelors: Lord Edward Innes-Ker, son of the Duke of Roxburghe; and with George Percy, the Earl Percy, Son of the Duke of Northumberland. Pippa and Kate's aristocratic friendships stemmed from their privileged education at Marlborough and the fact that they were fun, lively company. In certain circles, inspired no doubt by jealousy, the Middleton sisters were unkindly referred to as 'The Wysteria Sisters' because they were beautiful, fragrant and determined climbers. Such catty comments do not appear to

Opposite clockwise from top left: James Middleton (middle) enjoying a trip to Warwick Castle; skiing in Courchevel, France with Prince William and Kate in 2010; graduating from Edinburgh University in 2007

have troubled Pippa at all. She graduated from Edinburgh with an Honours degree in 2007.

Ironically, given that her sister would become the main event at the wedding of the century, in 2008 Pippa went to work for a company in London called Table Talk, an events management company that organises venues, catering, music, guest lists – everything you need, in fact, for anything from a private dinner or the opening of a gallery to a spectacular birthday party or even a wedding. She now divides her time between Table Talk and The Party Times, an online magazine she established to help promote her parents' company.

Like her sister, Pippa enjoys shooting, is a keen skier and in 2009 went tobogganing on the Cresta Run in St Moritz. Her glamorous lifestyle has included dating some high-profile young gentlemen including banking heir Jonathan Jardine Paterson, Alexander Spencer Churchill and former England cricketer Alex Loudon and she was once voted by *Tatler* magazine 'The No 1 Society Singleton'.

Pippa will need to use all of her organisational skills to marshal her team of 'little helpers' on her sister's wedding day as she will be in charge of bridesmaids Grace van Cutsem (Prince William's goddaughter), aged three; Eliza Lopes, also aged three; Lady Louise Windsor (Prince William's cousin), aged seven; The Hon. Margarita Armstrong-Jones, aged eight; and pageboys Tom Pettifer (Prince William's godson), aged eight; and William Lowther-Pinkerton (son of William's protection officer), aged ten.

For someone with Pippa Middleton's energy and enthusiasm, keeping the team of young attendants in line should pose no problems, but if there were any, her dazzling smile would cover a multitude of minor mishaps!

Opposite clockwise from top left: Pippa was voted 'No 1 Society Singleton' by *Tatler*; at a charity event with Isabella Calthorpe and Holly Branson, 2010; at the wedding of Katie Percy and Patrick Valentine, Feb 2011; chatting with Prince Harry on the polo field in 2009

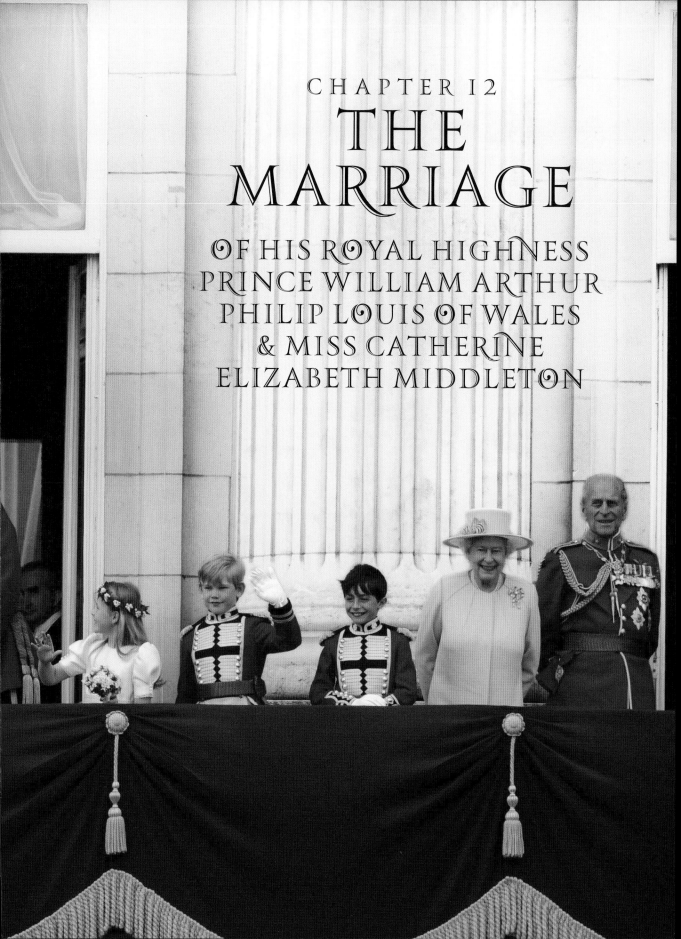

CHAPTER 12
THE MARRIAGE

OF HIS ROYAL HIGHNESS PRINCE WILLIAM ARTHUR PHILIP LOUIS OF WALES & MISS CATHERINE ELIZABETH MIDDLETON

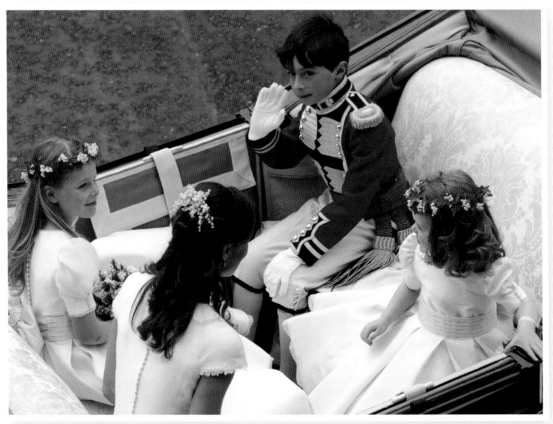